LEGEND —
TRAIL •••••
TELEGRAPH
LINE ———

AMISK LAKE

CUMBERLAND HOUSE

NORWAY HOUSE

PARROT R.

PASQUIA HILLS

RED DEER R.

CEDAR LK.

LAKE

WINNIPEG

PORCUPINE HILLS

LIVINGSTONE

LAKE WINNIPEGOSIS

SWAN LAKE

DUCK MTNS

FT. PELLY

BEAVER HILLS

RIDING MTN

MANITOBA

QU'APPELLE

QU'APPELLE R.

FT. ELLICE

SHOAL LAKE

ASSINIBOINE R.

MINNEDOSA

SELKIRK

FT. GARRY

QU'APPELLE

PIPESTONE CR.

BRANDON

PORTAGE LA PRAIRIE

RED R.

MOOSE MTN.

SOURIS R.

SOURIS R.

TURTLE MTN.

FIRST MERIDIAN

SECOND MERIDIAN

Ralph C. Russell 1896 - 1964

Ralph C. Russell moved from Ontario with his family to a Saskatchewan homestead when he was nine years old. There he was introduced to the old prairie trails that at one time were the "highways" of the west. They triggered an interest in pioneer history that was to stay with him throughout his life. He has published many articles about the Prairies' early days. This book is the culmination of his constant research.

THE
CARLTON TRAIL

The Broad Highway into the Saskatchewan Country
From the Red River Settlement
1840 - 1880

R. C. Russell

PRAIRIE BOOKS
THE WESTERN PRODUCER
SASKATOON
1971

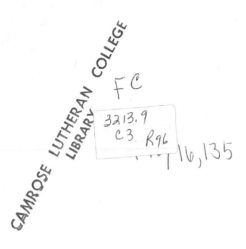
First Edition, 1955
Second (Revised) Edition, 1971

Permission to use the material on the Rev. Andrew Baird, which was published in an article in *The Beaver,* Winter, 1959, was obtained from the publishers.

PRAIRIE BOOKS SERVICE
THE WESTERN PRODUCER
SASKATOON, SASKATCHEWAN

Printed and Bound in Canada
by Modern Press

ISBN 919306-30-6

PREFACE

The author's interest in old prairie trails dates back to the year 1906, when his father homesteaded a quarter section of land situated about eighteen miles north of Lipton, Saskatchewan.

In those days there was not a mile of straight road between that town and our homestead. We followed the Touchwood Trail, with its accompanying telegraph line, for about twelve miles, then branched off on the North Trail that led to the Birch Lake district. After following it for about five miles we blazed a brand new trail to our prairie home.

The Touchwood Trail passed about four miles to the west of our homestead and the old Carlton Trail passed about eight miles northeast of us. The two trails joined each other on the edge of the Touchwood Hills a short distance northwest of the site where the town of Lestock now stands. For a number of years I saw considerable traffic passing along the Touchwood Trail. It consisted of wagons, democrats and buggies drawn by horses or oxen, and many of the wagons were piled high with settlers' effects. While the Grand Trunk Pacific Railway was being built through the eastern part of the Touchwood Hills district a great amount of "freighting" was done along this trail. But the Carlton Trail was almost entirely deserted when I first saw it.

In later years I made the acquaintance of the Carlton Trail in the Humboldt and Duck Lake districts. As I learned more about its history, I became fascinated with tales of happenings that took place along its course and finally decided to write the story of this trail as a hobby. My earnest hope is that my readers will derive as much pleasure as I have from the stories that I gleaned from various books relating to the Carlton Trail, and that the excerpts from these books, contained in the following story, will stimulate my readers to hunt up the original books and peruse many of them in their entirety. With this thought in mind a complete list of these books and shorter articles is appended at the end of my story of the Trail. They are referred to by number throughout the text.

A brief discussion is included of several events that affected the history of the Carlton Trail more or less directly. These include the construction of the first telegraph line across the Prairie Provinces, the coming of the North West Mounted Police, the surveying of the land for settlement, the building of the first transcontinental railway in Canada, and the Riel Rebellion of 1885.

Although the main emphasis in this booklet is laid on the story of the Carlton Trail and not on the history of the Prairie Provinces, great care has been taken to present historical matters accurately.

R.C.R., 1955

ACKNOWLEDGMENTS

The author wishes to express his sincere thanks to several individuals and organizations who contributed to the production of this booklet.

Mr. A. J. Loveridge, Grenfell, Sask., generously contributed an account of his experiences as a lad on a survey party in 1882. Mr. George Shepherd, Saskatoon, supplied several priceless photographs taken around Fort Walsh about 1878. I am indebted to Mr. R. J. Ledingham, Saskatoon, for Figure 6, to Mr. Rowan Glen, Punnichy, for Figure 29, and to Mr. Wm. J. McDonald, Yorkton, for Figure 37. The trustees of Riverlot School District, Carlton, Sask., kindly gave me permission to include Figure 31. My daughter, Lorna, designed the cover.

I am greatly indebted to the various writers and publishers listed in the bibliography for parts of the text material and for three of the figures.

In the matter of the publication and distribution of this booklet, the author is grateful for the constant interest and support of Professor G. W. Simpson, head of the Department of History, University of Saskatchewan, and the Jubilee Publications Committee, of which he is chairman. Finally my hearty thanks are due to the Agricultural Graduates Association of our university, for assistance in the early distribution of *The Carlton Trail*.

R.C.R., 1955

R. C. RUSSELL
1896-1964

INTRODUCTION

One can be acquainted with a man for a long time without actually having discovered him; and I wish I had discovered Ralph Russell earlier. After a few years of more or less casual acquaintance, I found myself on the first ōf many memorable hunting trips in his company. It was then that the rewarding experience of discovery began. Ostensibly, our object was to shoot ducks and prairie chickens, but I was soon to realize that as far as Ralph was concerned, this was little more than a front for satisfying a deeper and undoubtedly more elevating urge.

He had two great over-riding hobbies, and he carried them both with him wherever he went. One of these was delving into pioneer history, the story of the opening-up and settling of the Great Plains country of the Canadian West. For Ralph Russell had himself experienced the receding edge of that momentous period. At the impressionable age of nine years, he had accompanied his parents in their move from the little village of Charing Cross in southwestern Ontario, to settle on a Saskatchewan homestead. Here he was intrigued by the deep-rutted winding freight trails which provided the only means of travel and communication over the unfenced prairie. He was never to outgrow the lure of these trails and the adventures that were enacted upon them.

But it was not within his nature to be satisfied with having seen a segment of the historic Carlton Trail before it fell into complete disuse. Throughout the rest of his life he must follow it, seach it out wherever its remains could still be found, question oldtime residents for scraps of information, consult archivists, visit historians and librarians, dig up bits and pieces of the story from every conceivable source, and then put them all together and produce his book as a contribution to Saskatchewan's Golden Jubilee celebrations. Here is recounted every noteworthy journey and event in which the great trail played a part, that the researches of this painstaking author could bring to light.

Nor was he satisfied simply to discover and record the bare facts of history. He must bring them back to life, and spill his enthusiasm among groups of friends in day-long tours, scouting out the exact spots where history was made, and matching the still-existing landmarks with those recorded by the original participants whom he re-injected into the scene with on-the-spot readings from their journals and reports.

His other main hobby, which proved to be a major influence in his professional career, was in the field of botany. He became a leading authority on the identification of Saskatchewan weeds and native plants; those which he was unable to recognize on sight, he made it his business to "run down" and add to his collection of pressed and mounted specimens. He also collected specimens demonstrating the important diseases which attack field and garden crops. These collections, which include also many of the common fungi, occupy a room in the Canada Department of Agriculture Research Station on the Saskatoon campus of the University of Saskatchewan. A sign on the door of this room, recently placed there by his colleagues, identifies it as "The Ralph C. Russell Herbarium," and a plaque within pays fitting tribute to his accomplishments.

It should also be noted that Dr. Russell was a principal co-author of "An Annotated List of the Plants of Saskatchewan" which, along with the herbarium, is used as a standard reference by all prairie botanists and plant pathologists.

But botany, pioneer history, and the Carlton Trail were only a part of Ralph Russell's varied life and interests. After training as a Royal Air Force pilot in the closing year of the first world war, he entered the University of Saskatchewan where he obtained the degrees of Bachelor of Science in Agriculture (1924), and Master of Science (1926). Later, he continued his studies at the University of Toronto, where he was awarded the degree of Doctor of Philosophy in 1934.

In the meantime, he had embarked upon his professional career as a plant pathologist at the Canada Department of Agriculture Research Station in Saskatoon. Here, his research into diseases of cereal crops led to the publication of many papers in scientific journals and farm magazines.

Perhaps among his many contributions to the betterment of agriculture, Dr. Russell will be remembered best for his research on the destructive "take-all" disease of wheat, in which he pointed up the usefulness of certain crop rotational methods for its control. He also developed a practical method of overcoming smut in the production of certified seed barley. The economic value of such work in the grain-growing industry, is beyond estimation.

Upon his retirement in 1961, Dr. R. C. Russell was made an Honorary Life Member of the Canadian Seed Growers' Association, in recognition of his distinguished service.

C. G. RILEY, Ph. D.
formerly officer-in-charge, Forest Pathology Laboratory for Saskatchewan and Manitoba, Canada Department of Forestry, Saskatoon. May, 1971

TABLE OF CONTENTS

ILLUSTRATIONS

THE CARLTON TRAIL

Among the many winding trails that crisscrossed the plains and parklands of the Northwest Territories during the four decades preceding the advent of the transcontinental railway, none was more important than the Carlton Trail, also known as the Saskatchewan Trail. A great deal of romance is bound up in the written and unwritten records of these old trails. The Carlton Trail led across plain and marsh, hill and dale, coulee, creek, and river, from Fort Garry, at the junction of the Red and the Assiniboine rivers, to Fort Carlton, more than five hundred miles to the northwest, on the bank of the North Saskatchewan River. Fort Carlton stood on the east side of that river at a point about fifteen miles west of the present town of Duck Lake.

The principal vehicle used on the Carlton Trail was the Red River cart (Fig. 1). This was a two-wheeled vehicle of wood. No metal was used in its construction, although shaganappi (green buffalo hide) was used to some extent to bind its parts together. The cart had a pair of shafts between which to place the ox or pony that was to haul it, and a rectangular rack with a floor of planking balanced on the axle. At times a canvas cover was put over the rack to protect passengers or perishable freight from rain or snow. In some cases a covering was thrown over the cart and the owner slept on the ground beneath it when camping at night.

When freighters were traveling along the trail with long strings of heavily loaded carts, each man looked after several units, a unit consisting of one pony or ox and one cart. Each freighter drove the animal hitched to his leading cart and tied the next succeeding animal to a rear corner of this cart, so that the animal walked in the rut of the wheel in front of it. Each succeeding animal under the driver's care followed in the wheel track of the cart immediately ahead. As a result of this arrangement, the carts did not travel in a single line but were spread out

1

so that the trail consisted of as many as sixteen ruts all worn to about the same depth. This method reduced the danger of the ruts becoming too deep for convenient use and lessened the chances of getting stuck in wet spots on the prairie. The old cart trails differed in appearance from the trails made at a later date by wagons, buckboards and buggies. The latter trails consisted of two wheel marks and a path for single horses between them (Fig. 2).

The route followed by the Carlton Trail is shown on the map (Fig. 3). It started out along what is now Portage Avenue in Winnipeg and followed the north bank of the Assiniboine River fairly closely until it reached Portage la Prairie. This portion of the trail passed over low-lying plains dotted with occasional sloughs and intersected by a few creeks flowing into the Assiniboine River. During wet seasons the trail here led across many "sloughs of despond," and woeful tales were told of carts becoming stuck in the tenacious mud, and of their owners having to unload them and "double up" their ponies or oxen to pull their carts from the bogs before reloading their possessions.

According to the map contained in the book *Description of the Province of Manitoba* (5), the trail branched at Portage la Prairie into two alternative routes for the next ninety miles or so. The southern branch continued on in a westerly direction for about twenty miles and then veered slightly to the southwest as it passed through the district around the sources of Squirrel Creek and Pine Creek. This branch appears to have followed an old buffalo-hunting trail for some distance. The latter proceeded on to the place where Brandon now stands, then turning in a southwesterly direction it ran across country to a bend in the Souris River, from whence it passed on to the plains along the Missouri River. The southern branch of the Carlton Trail departed from the old hunting trail near the west side of section 7, township 11, range 8, west of the first meridian. From this

2

F<small>IG</small>. 1—*Explorer's camp near the elbow of the North Saskatchewan River. Note the two Red River carts, one of which is provided with a canvas cover.*

point it traveled in a northwesterly direction, passing about two miles west of Gregg, a station on the main line of the Canadian National Railway, about midway between Portage la Prairie and Rivers, Manitoba. Continuing in a northwesterly direction, it crossed the White Mud River near Oberon, and the Minnedosa River (then known as the Little Saskatchewan) about four miles west of the present town of Minnedosa. It rejoined the northern branch of the trail approximately twenty miles west and five miles north of that town.

The northern branch traveled northwesterly from Portage la Prairie to Westbourne. Then veering to the west it passed close to Woodside and Gladstone. In doing so it crossed the White Mud River three times. About twelve miles west of Gladstone it swung to the north for several miles, to avoid a bend in the White Mud, and then passed three miles north of

3

Neepawa and crossed the Little Saskatchewan River two miles northeast of Minnedosa.

From Portage la Prairie to Fort Ellice the trail traversed a considerable amount of rising land and crossed several creeks and rivers flowing either north and east toward Lake Manitoba, or south toward the Assiniboine. Some of these streams flowed through relatively deep valleys with abrupt slopes at the edges, which were difficult to ascend or descend with heavily loaded carts. Although these streams did not constitute formidable barriers in times of low water, they were real hazards when they were in flood. In this stretch the trail mounted from the level of the first prairie steppe to that of the second, climbing from an altitude of about 700 feet above sea level in the Red River Valley to an altitude of about 1,600 feet at Fort Ellice. At this point the trail branched again for a short distance. The left branch crossed the Assiniboine River below its junction with the Qu'Appelle and called at Fort Ellice, a Hudson's Bay Company post, built on the plateau a mile or so west of the Assiniboine Valley near a deep coulee through which Beaver Creek entered the Assiniboine River. The right branch crossed the Assiniboine above its junction with the Qu'Appelle. These branches were reunited on section 14-17-29, west of the first meridian, at a point about four miles northwest of Fort Ellice. As both the Assiniboine and Qu'Appelle valleys were about 250 feet deep, and both had very steep sides, descending into them and climbing out again was arduous work, especially with heavily loaded carts.

From Fort Ellice the trail followed a northwesterly course to the Touchwood Hills. In later years the Grand Trunk Pacific Railway followed nearly the same route as far as the town of Lestock, near the third Touchwood Hills trading post of the Hudson's Bay Company. Melville was built about two and one-half miles north of the Carlton Trail and several towns along this railway lie practically on the trail.

4

From the Touchwood Hills the trail veered more to the north and passed fairly close to where Lanigan, Humboldt and Wakaw now stand. It crossed the South Saskatchewan River at Batoche.

In the Touchwood Hills some of the hilltops rise to an altitude of over 2,300 feet. The trail crossed the saline Quill Plains about twelve miles southwest of Big Quill Lake. The flat area was frequently referred to as the Great Salt Plains, but as Macoun (21) pointed out, this name gives an exaggerated impression of the extent of the non-arable land within this area. Here again travelers expended a great deal of energy and profanity struggling through the mosquito-infested marshes in wet seasons. However, as compensations, the country between the

FIG. 2—*Prairie trail in the Touchwood Hills district. The bluff is composed mainly of trembling poplar (aspen) and several shrubby species of willow.*

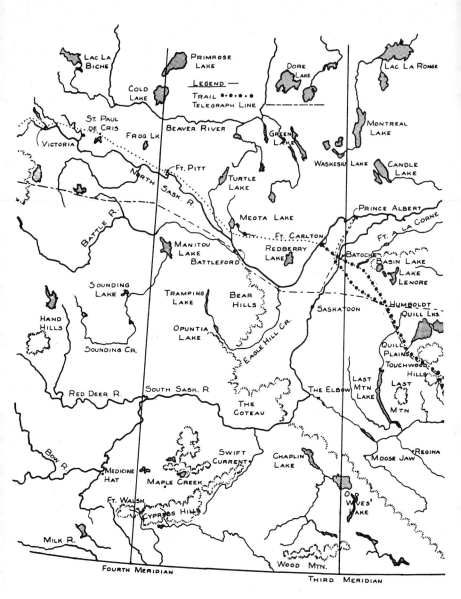

FIG. 3—*Map depicting a portion of Western Canada before the Prairie Provinces were formed. The route followed by the Carlton Trail, connecting Fort Garry and Fort Carlton, is shown, and also the continuation of this trail to a point just beyond the Indian Mission called Victoria, that lay on the way to Edmonton. Branches of the*

6

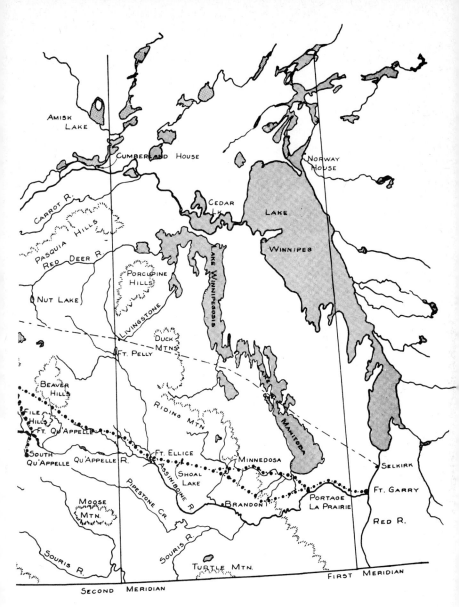

Carlton Trail, leading to Prince Albert and to South Qu'Appelle
are indicated. In addition, the Dominion Government's telegraph
line from Selkirk to Edmonton is marked, with its branches from
Humboldt to South Qu'Appelle and from Clark's Crossing to
Prince Albert.

Touchwood post and Batoche offered many fine vistas from the higher places along the way (Fig. 4); miles and miles of rich pasture land stretching away in level or rolling expanses to the distant horizon, dotted with plenty of bluffs to supply fuel and protection from the wind and usually with numerous sloughs (ponds or marshes) of water to refresh man and beast at the camping places.

The last major obstacle before reaching Fort Carlton was the mighty South Saskatchewan River. True, the Hudson's Bay Company usually kept a boat at Batoche in which travelers could ferry their goods across the river, but the horses and oxen had to swim for it. Also, the boat had to be tracked upstream some distance before starting across for the opposite shore because the strong current carried it rapidly downstream while it was being rowed across. In flood times, or when the ice was beginning to form in the autumn or breaking up in the springtime, crossing this river was a very dangerous venture. Having crossed the river, an easy stage led through sandy parklands to Fort Carlton (Fig. 5). The first fort on this site was built in 1810, and the last fort was destroyed by fire during the rebellion of 1885. For several decades it was one of the principal posts of the Hudson's Bay Company. Being on the main waterway and also on the main land route across Rupert's Land, it was visited by many people both great and humble.

In later years a branch of the Carlton Trail was formed between Humboldt and Duck Lake. It followed a more southerly route. It passed close to the sites of Bruno and Bremen, and crossed the South Saskatchewan at Gabriel's Crossing. This ferrying point was named after Riel's lieutenant, Gabriel Dumont, who operated its ferry for a time. From this point the trail swung to the north and rejoined the older route near Duck Lake. Some of the people to whom we shall refer crossed the river at Batoche and others crossed it at Gabriel's Crossing, depending on which branch of the trail they followed.

8

FIG. 4—*Rolling parkland near Dana, Sask. The south branch of the Carlton Trail passed within a few miles of Dana.*

The Carlton Trail and the creaking Red River cart bore much the same relationship to the Saskatchewan country as did the Oregon Trail and the covered wagon to the Pacific Northwest region of the United States. The genesis of this trail goes back some distance in history to early developments of the fur trade in the vast region then known as Rupert's Land. For some time after the formation of the Hudson's Bay Company in 1670, it had trading posts on the shores of Hudson Bay, but none inland. Consequently, the Indians who dealt with the Company had to travel from their own hunting grounds to the shore of the Bay in order to take their furs to the Company's posts, which entailed a great loss of time and many hardships for the Indians who lived far inland. By about 1750 the French fur traders from the St. Lawrence had pentrated to the Northwest, through what is now western Manitoba and eastern Saskatchewan, as far as Fort à la Corne, and had cut off much of the trade from the

9

English posts on the Bay. Even after Canada became a British possession in 1763 private traders and large organizations, such as the North West Company, continued to penetrate Rupert's Land and to compete for the Indians' furs. It was not until 1774 that the Hudson's Bay Company shook off its lethargy and commenced erecting inland posts or forts at which the Indians could trade with comparative ease. This system of posts gradually spread over the forests and prairie to the Rocky Mountains, and even beyond these to the Pacific Ocean.

In order to supply trading goods to the posts east of the Rocky Mountains and bring back furs to York Factory, the company hired Scotsmen, Métis, and Indians to man brigades

FIG. 5—*Fort Carlton as it appeared in 1872, with the North Saskatchewan River in the background. The fort stood on a level bench about twenty feet above the level of the river and a hundred feet below the plateau to the east of the bench.*

of York boats and canoes to carry these commodities back and forth. In this way it built up a remarkable transportation system, which continued to function until the approach of railways and steamboats through Minnesota made it easier to bring in goods and take out hides and furs by a new route. The York Factory route was not abandoned by the Churchill and Athabaska River brigades until 1872 (33). During the transition period, starting about 1860, more and more of the transporting was accomplished by means of Red River carts carrying the furs and buffalo hides down to Fort Garry and taking back supplies to the trading posts, largely over the Carlton Trail. In 1867, according to Father Lacombe, 114 carts passed through his Métis settlement at St. Paul de Cris carrying supplies to the Hudson's Bay post at Edmonton. However, the servants of the company were not the only people who made use of the trail connecting Fort Garry with Fort Carlton. Métis from the Red River Settlement, seeking buffalo (American bison) on the plains of the Northwest, or moving to new homes along the branches of the Saskatchewan River, followed it for various distances. Private traders, missionaries, explorers, Mounted Policemen, governmental dignitaries, and even tourists and sportsmen from far countries traveled it at one time or another. Many of them continued on beyond Carlton to Edmonton or even over the mountains to the Pacific Ocean. Also, many miners from Eastern Canada, bound for the gold fields of British Columbia, chose this overland route rather than the long voyage by sea. Finally, the land surveyors and the early tide of ranchers and farmers, entering the fertile districts which stretched on either side of the great trail throughout its entire length, used it to a greater or lesser extent. Extracts from the written records of diverse individuals from this motley throng are included in this account to provide an authentic impression of conditions as they existed in this part of the Canadian Northwest nearly a century ago.

11

THE MÉTIS AND THEIR BUFFALO HUNTS

It is hard to say who first created the Carlton Trail. In all probability the eastern portion came into being some time before the whole route was established. Probably some of the Métis of the Red River Settlement marked it out in a westerly direction, as far as Fort Ellice, while going to the country along the south side of the Qu'Appelle Valley to hunt buffalo. Later they may have continued it in a northwesterly direction through the Touchwood Hills to hunt on the Quill Plains. On the other hand, employees of the Hudson's Bay Company may have been the first to mark out this overland route between Fort Garry and Fort Carlton, as an alternative to the water route via Lake Winnipeg and the Saskatchewan River. Sir George Simpson made a trip overland from Fort Carlton to Fort Garry in the spring of 1825, but the Carlton Trail was not yet established

Fig. 6—*Buffalo bull at rest on the plain. Many of the Indians and Métis of Rupert's Land secured their livelihood by hunting buffalo.*

12

and he passed north of the Quill Lakes and turned south to Fort Ellice after reaching the upper part of the Assiniboine River (31). However, it is known that some of the Métis did go from the Red River Settlement to the districts mentioned in search of buffalo (Fig. 6), while others went west to the Missouri Coteau or southwest to the Missouri River to hunt. Also, some Métis frequented the country around Fort Carlton with goods to trade to the Indians for furs. Dr. Hector, one of Captain Palliser's party, speaking of the Thickwood Cree whom he met in the winter of 1857-58 twenty miles northwest of Carlton, wrote (37):

> They, for the most part, trade at Fort Carlton, but a great deal of the large quantities of fur which they annually trap has of late years been diverted from the Company by free traders, parties of whom from the Red River spend the winter among the Indians, well supplied with goods, which are furnished to them by the American traders. This rival trading on the whole would be good for the Indians, were it not for the wretched poisonous whiskey which is supplied to them.

From 1868 on, numbers of Métis families moved from the Red River district to the South Saskatchewan River and settled along its banks from Fish Creek to St. Louis.

Let us pull the curtain aside and look at the romantic life that these semi-nomads led during the summer hunt on the plains. The following description of a buffalo hunt that occurred in 1850, taken from the book *Father Lacombe* (13), refers to the hunt organized at Pembina:

> This was the Golden Age of the Indians and Métis when the bison still roamed the plains in unnumbered thousands. The tender buffalo meat, dried fresh and pounded, made a good food both appetizing and nutritious; the buffalo skins made robes for garments and bedding, hides for teepees and canoes; while on the unwooded plains the sun-dried manure served the purpose for fuel.
>
> It fell to Father Lacombe's lot to be chaplain of the great hunt in 1850. He was alive to the pleasures and novelty of his new assignment, for all about him the preparations of his people were tinged with joyousness and excitement . . .

13

The Métis of the area were finally all assembled and ready to organize for the hunt:

No order had been observed up to this time in their mode of arrival or their preparation but Voila! how the scene changes! the fine discipline of a military camp suddenly pervaded the assembly. The hunters held a council to select, by a majority of votes, a chief and ten captains, who in turn selected ten or fifteen others to act as scouts. Then they drew up anew the laws of the hunt . . . The halfbreed hunter, Wilkie, who had been elected chief, rose at the close of the council and asked for the hunters' acceptance of these laws as a whole. This being done by a majority of voices the chief declared solemnly: "If any among you do not approve of these laws, let him leave our camp and come not with us, for once we have set out together from this encampment no one will be free to separate from us."

No man left the assembly; they silently approved of its laws. These related to the time and mode of chasing the buffalo and to the penalties fixed for the infringement of any of these laws.

After an early Mass next morning the signal of departure was given by the guide of the day with a little flag. In an instant a great commotion ran through the whole camp. The lodges of skin and the tents were pulled down, the horses were brought into a corral from the prairie, and the women made haste to pack into the carts their small household goods. Then the women and children took seats in the carts, the hunters mounted their buffalo runners, and the camp set out on its march. There were from 800 to 1,000 carts in the camp that year, and over 1,000 men, women and children, as well as hundreds of fine ponies for buffalo runners, besides cart horses, oxen and innumerable dogs.

Close to the sixth day out the Métis' long lines drew near to the Turtle Mountains. Scouts pushing on ahead saw in the distance an immense herd of buffalo and signaled the good news to their party:

The information flashed back by the flags was intoxicating. Joy ran through the whole regiment of marching Métis, and the buffalo ponies, keen for the hunt as their masters were, understood the

14

sudden commotion and halt. In a trice the women, children, and old men dragged out the lodgepoles and skins and erected the camp.

The hunting ponies were led aside, swiftly mounted, and in full gallop they flashed along the prairie to the ridge on which the scouts had paused.

On the green rolling prairies stretching before them to the horizon buffalo were grazing, thousands of them, forming a billowy black lake on the prairie.

The captains gave the word and the hunters instantly fell into one long line of attack. "En avant!" the leader cried, and men and horses flew forward with whirlwind velocity. Now the buffalo broke into confused flight as the hunters strove to catch up with them. These hunts were filled with marvels of horsemanship, for the hunters urged their ponies right into the lumbering herd of buffalo, because they usually picked out the better animals as targets and rode right up beside them before firing. Apart from the danger of the horses stumbling in badger holes and throwing their masters in the path of the stampeding herd, the wounded bulls sometimes charged horses and riders and occasionally injured them severely. ,

As the hunters prepared to shoot they dropped the reins and guided their ponies by pressure of their limbs only. Each hunter carried a powder horn at his belt and bullets in his mouth. He discharged and reloaded his flintlock musket with remarkable dexterity, when it is considered that during these operations his horse was on the gallop, keeping up with the fleeing buffalo. Sometimes in the hunter's haste he fired his gun when the bullet was not in contact with the powder and then the gun barrel was apt to burst and maim the hunter. On this particular occasion hundreds of buffalo were killed but there were no serious accidents to the hunters.

The turmoil of the hunt was scarcely over before the stillness of the plains was broken by a new, lighter clamour — delighted women and children hastening from the camp with carts drawn by old ponies to haul back the spoils.

15

The dead animals were then skinned and cut up. The meat and hides were loaded on the carts and the remains were left for the numerous wolves which always gathered at the scene of a hunt.

In picturesque disorder the party made its way back through the cool of the evening air to the fires of the camp by the Turtle Mountains. The meat had been piled on the creaking carts by the women and hunters, and the latter with their labours concluded, walked beside their tired mounts or rode them at a gentle lope over the prairies, preceding the carts and the women-folk. At the camp they turned the ponies free. The hunters sat about the fires, smoking and living the brief, wild hunt over again. Meanwhile the women picked out the choicest bits of fresh meat and cooked a savoury meal for their lords.

The camp remainded at this point for several days, while the women, after the centuries-old fashion of their sex, dressed the buffalo skins and dried the meat. They first cut up the meat in very long strips which they stretched to dry on scaffolds made of young trees. After two or three days' exposure to the sun the meat was sufficiently dry for the women to fold it into packages tightly bound with sinew. Then with their stone mallets they pounded the dried meat to powder in wooden bowls, mixing hot grease and dried berries with it, packed the whole into large sacs of buffalo-hide, called by the Métis taureaux. This was pimikkan [sic], the manna of the Canadian prairies.

After several weeks of traveling and alternately hunting and preserving buffalo meat, these people usually returned to their homes in the settlements along the Red River. There they farmed, in a half-hearted and leisurely fashion, until the fall hunt took place. Much of their harvest of pemmican and hides was exchanged with the traders for the commodities which the latter had to barter.

According to numerous authorities similar hunts were conducted hundreds of times, by the Métis or Indians in different parts of Rupert's Land, during the next twenty-five years. The pemmican and dried meat, secured in this way, not only served to sustain the hunters and their families, but also many of the employees of the Hudson's Bay Company. The Company purchased great quantities of pemmican or had it made by Indians and half-breeds in its employ. Even the men of the posts and brigades far to the north subsisted largely on pemmican.

EMIGRANTS TO THE COLUMBIA RIVER VALLEY

It is recorded that in the year 1841 a party of Red River people, under the guidance of Pierre Dunomais, journeyed from Fort Garry to Fort Carlton on the first lap of their overland trip to find new homes in the valley of the Columbia River beyond the mountains. Sir George Simpson, Governor of the Hudson's Bay Company, with his own party of about eighteen men with thirty-six horses and four carts, followed in their wake. They caught up with the emigrants about half way between Fort Carlton and Fort Pitt. The following is Simpson's description of the emigrant party (39):

> These emigrants consisted of agriculturists and others, principally natives of Red River settlement. There were twenty-three families, the heads being generally young and active, though a few of them were advanced in life, more particularly one poor woman, upwards of seventy-five years of age, who was tottering after her son to his new home. This venerable wanderer was a native of the Saskatchewan, the name of which, in fact, she bore. She had been absent from this the land of her birth for eighteen years; and, on catching the first glimpse of the river, from the hill near Carlton, she burst, under the influence of old recollections, into a violent flood of tears. During the two days that the party spent at the fort, she scarcely ever left the bank of the stream, appearing to regard it with as much veneration as the Hindoo regards the Ganges.

> As a contrast to this superannuated daughter of the Saskatchewan, the band contained several very young travellers, who had, in fact, made their appearance in this world since the commencement of the journey. Beyond the inevitable detention which seldom exceeded a few hours, these interesting events had never interfered with the progress of the brigade; and both mother and child used to jog on, as if jogging were the condition of human existence.

17

Each family had two or three carts, together with a band of horses, cattle, and dogs. The men and lads travelled on the saddle, while the vehicles, which were covered with awnings against the sun and rain, carried the women and children. As they marched in single file, their cavalcade extended above a mile in length; and we increased the length of the column by marching in company. The emigrants were all healthy and happy, living in the greatest abundance and enjoying the journey with the highest relish.

SIR GEORGE SIMPSON

Apparently the party of emigrants had little to follow in the way of a trail from Fort Ellice to Fort Carlton, for Simpson wrote, "As these people were pursuing the same route as ourselves, and would beat a good track, we resolved, as far as practicable, to follow their trail."

Even at that early date the Simpson party found batteaux at the crossings of the Assiniboine and South Saskatchewan rivers, in which they were able to ferry their goods and their persons across those streams, but he speaks of having to ford the Qu'Appelle River (Fig. 7.).

FIG. 7—*The Qu'Appelle River. Fording this stream was no easy matter.*

18

Sir George Simpson had an eye for beauty. On several occasions he remarked on the appearance or the perfume of various native flowers such as the "tiger lily" (Lilium umbellatum Pursh), later to become the official floral emblem of Saskatchewan, the "blue bell" (Campanula petiolata A.DC.), and the "rose" (of which there are several native species). He also speaks of the graceful antelopes and the other deer, and of the numerous species of birds seen along the way. He and his party met with a few Indians on this part of their journey, who either fled from the white men in fright or hung around and pestered them for presents, but they saw no buffalo until after they passed Fort Carlton. At times the mosquitoes attacked both men and horses mercilessly, but on the whole the traveling was pleasant when the weather was fine. At times, when it rained, they suffered great discomfort:

Next morning we marched till ten o'clock in a soaking rain. An encampment in such weather is by no means an exhilarating sight. On halting we were wet and chilly, but had no place to shelter ourselves from the shower. After a drawn battle of nearly an hour with the wind and rain in the way of making a fire, we at last succeeded; and then heaping on whole piles of wood, we contrived to keep ourselves tolerably comfortable till our tents were pitched. The horses were the very picture of misery, as they huddled themselves together. To all this add drooping spirits and a murky sky, and you have a pretty correct idea of that kind of picnic breakfast on which the clouds drop their fatness.

Finally, Simpson's party reached Fort Carlton:

A smart ride of four or five hours from the Bow River [South Saskatchewan], through a country very much resembling an English park, brought us to Fort Carlton, on the Saskatchewan, where we found every soul in the establishment enjoying a siesta with open gates — a conclusive proof of either the carelessness of our people or the peaceful disposition of the neighboring savages. Our day's work had been remarkable, almost to a ludicrous degree, from the number of falls that we encountered, for each of us had a roll or two on the turf, so harmless, however, as not to leave a single bruise to boast of. Besides the exhausted state of our

19

horses, the ground was drilled into a honeycomb by badger holes, which, being pretty well screened by grass at this season of the year, could seldom be discerned soon enough to be avoided.

At Carlton, we took up our quarters for a couple of nights. We accomplished about six hundred miles in thirteen days — a fair rate of travelling, considering that many of our horses had come the whole distance heavily laden. This fort stands in latitude 53° N.; it is in the form of a lozenge, being surrounded by wooden stockades of considerable height, with bastions at each angle and over the gateway. In the immediate vicinity, there are large gardens and fields, which produce abundance of potatoes and other vegetables; but wheat, though it has sometimes succeeded, has been far more frequently destroyed by the early frosts of autumn, which even on the Red River, occasionally blight the hopes of the less active among the settlers.

Here, we leave Simpson to pursue his romatic journey across the continent, and turn to the experiences of others who traveled the trail in later years. There occurs a blank period of about sixteen years between Simpson's account and the next written records of the Carlton Trail. It is not known, for certain, who utilized the trail and marked it more distinctly during this period, but it seems probable that officials of the Hudson's Bay Company used it occasionally. Also, it is likely that buffalo hunters and free traders from the Red River Settlement followed it to and from the Saskatchewan country.

PAUL KANE

We can obtain glimpses of what was going on at Fort Garry and Fort Carlton, a few years after Sir George Simpson's famous journey, from the writings of Paul Kane (15). This remarkable individual came to Canada from Ireland in his boyhood and settled in Toronto. On attaining his manhood he chose art as his vocation. After traveling for some years in the United States and studying in various parts of Europe he returned to Canada and decided to devote his energy and talent to studying and depicting the Indians of Canada and their way of life.

After spending one season on this work in western Ontario, he journeyed to Fort Garry and across Rupert's Land to the Pacific Coast and back, with the help of the Hudson's Bay Company. In the course of his long journey, which took him from May, 1846, to October, 1848, he came in contact with many Indian tribes. Besides making dozens of sketches illustrating the leading Indian chiefs, and the costumes, weapons, and activities of their tribesmen, he collected a great deal of information about their customs and brought back many articles of their dress and equipment. Many of these articles and paintings are still preserved in the Royal Ontario Museum.

On the outward journey he went out with a party of half-breed residents of the Red River Settlement and hunted buffalo with them for a time on the plains of the Missouri River region. Then he returned to Fort Garry and traveled by boat to Norway House. From this post he crossed the north end of Lake Winnipeg and ascended the Saskatchewan by York boat to Fort Carlton. He relates an amusing incident which occurred there in September, 1846. It involved the Rev. Robert Rundle, a Wesleyan Methodist missionary after whom Mount Rundle, near Banff, was named:

Mr. Rundell [sic], a missionary, whose station was at Edmonton, was at Carlton awaiting our arrival, for the purpose of returning in company with us. He had with him a favourite cat which he had brought with him in the canoes from Edmonton, being afraid to leave her behind him, as there was some danger of her being eaten during his absence. This cat was the object of a good deal of amusement amongst the party, of great curiosity amongst the Indians, and a good deal of anxiety and trouble to its kind master.

Mr. Rowand, myself, and Mr. Rundell, having determined to proceed to Edmonton on horseback, as being the shortest and most agreeable route, we procured horses and a guide, and on the morning of the 12th of September we arose early for our start. The Indians had collected in numbers around the fort to see us off, and shake hands with us, a practice which they seem to have taken a particular fancy for. No sooner had we mounted our rather skittish animals than the Indians crowded around, and Mr. Rundell, who was rather a favourite amongst them, came in for a large share of their attentions, which seemed to be rather annoying to his horse. His cat he had tied to the pummel of his saddle by a string, about four feet long, around her neck, and had her safely, as he thought, concealed in the breast of his capote. She, however, did not relish the plunging of the horse, and made a spring out, utterly astonishing the Indians, who could not conceive where she had come from. The string brought her up against the horse's legs, which she immediately attacked. The horse now became furious, kicking violently, and at last threw Mr. Rundell over his head, but fortunately without much injury. All present were convulsed with laughter, to which the Indians added screeching and yelling as an accompaniment, rendering the whole scene indescribably ludicrous. Puss's life was saved by the string breaking; but we left her behind for the men to bring in the boats, evidently to the regret of her master, notwithstanding the hearty laugh which we had had at his expense.

On his return trip, Paul Kane went down the North Saskatchewan River with a brigade taking the furs out, in the spring of 1848. The brigade, when it left Edmonton, consisted of twenty-three boats and 130 men. It was under the command of a Mr. Harriett. Among the others included in the company was Monsig. de Merse, the Catholic Bishop of Vancouver. On their way down from Edmonton they stopped some distance below Fort Pitt to hold a confab with the head men of a huge war party of Blackfoot, Blood, Sarcee, and Piegan who were on their way to the Carlton district to attack the Cree. Among those of whom Paul Kane made portraits on this occasion, was a group of six chiefs. Two of these fell in the subsequent battle with the Cree.

The remainder of Kane's homeward journey through Rupert's Land passed without any startling incidents. He states that Bishop de Merse and his party left the brigade at Carlton and journeyed overland to the Red River Settlement. In doing this they doubtless followed the Carlton Trail. Farther down the river at The Pas, Kane met Sir John Richardson and

Dr. Rae on their way to the Mackenzie River Delta in search of Sir John Franklin's expedition. Paul Kane parted from the brigade and returned to the East via Lake Winnipeg and the Winnipeg River, so he did not go through Fort Garry on his way home.

CAPTAIN JOHN PALLISER

According to Palliser (37), a large party of emigrants from the Red River went out to the Columbia River Valley under the guidance of James Sinclair in 1855. In 1857 Palliser met a party of them at Fort Ellice, as they were returning to the Red River Settlement. James Sinclair had been killed by the Indians in the mountains. Palliser wrote:

> After this, many of the emigrants became discouraged, the prospects, quality, and extent of the land on the Columbia not being equal to their expectations. The bustling life and active business habits of the Americans with whom they came in contact were too much for them, and finally they determined to set off for Red River again, and had arrived thus far when we saw them. Their party consisted of about seven men, three women, and a few children, one of which had been born on the prairie and seemed to be doing remarkably well.

Captain Palliser was sent out, by the British Government, in charge of a small party of trained men to explore the comparatively unknown southwestern portion of Rupert's Land. This consisted mainly of the area between the present international boundary line and the north branch of the Saskatchewan River. He and his party spent much of the summers and falls of 1857-58-59 on this work. As his main object was the exploration of the unknown portions of the country, he did not make extensive use of the Carlton Trail. However, he sent one detachment with supplies for his expedition over it from Fort Garry to Fort Ellice in 1857. He returned over most of it with a small party in the autumn of the same year. From the Touchwood Hills, however, he took another trail to Fort Pelly, and then

23

came back to the Carlton Trail at Fort Ellice and followed it the rest of the way to Fort Garry. On the trip between Carlton and Touchwood the following entry was made in his diary:

October 13th — Saddled up and started at sunrise; made twelve miles before breakfast, for which we halted for one hour and a half; made ten miles, halted for dinner for another hour and half; rode fifteen miles further and camped. Country the same as yesterday, rich, rolling, and would have been well wooded but for fires. We discovered near camp the cause of the great fire which had occurred this autumn. It was kindled from the camp-fire of Mons. La Combe [sic], the Roman Catholic missionary to the Crees, on his way to Edmonton; this I learned from a notice planted there, in the shape of a post, on which was carved his initials and the date of the encampment in September.

The following spring Palliser returned from the East and traveled the full length of the Carlton Trail. He left Fort Garry on May the twelfth and arrived at Carlton on June the fifth. After describing the appearance of the country in early spring, and his impressions of its suitability for agricultural purposes, he speaks of his companions who had spent the winter in the Saskatchewan country and of the work which they had carried on in his absence:

On my arrival at Carlton, I found all the gentlemen under my command in good health. Doctor Hector, who has been in charge of the affairs of the expedition during my absence, had, in accordance with my instructions, hired men and purchased horses for the explorations of the ensuing summer; to carry out these objects it had been necessary for him to visit the Catholic settlement at Lake Ste. Ann's, fifty miles west from Edmonton. He therefore with most praiseworthy energy availed himself of this opportunity to lay down the whole of the North Saskatchewan, and visited Forts Pitt, Edmonton, and Rocky Mountain House, and even penetrated the flanking range of the Rocky Mountains during the winter.

Lieutenant Blakeston had joined the expedition shortly after my departure from Carlton last October [1857], and I found the magnetic observations under his instructions and conduct ably carried out, assisted by Mr. Sullivan and Mons. Bourgeau.

The numerous astronomical observations of Mr. Sullivan were all carefully recorded and submitted to me, as well as the computations and the results. Monsieur Bourgeau had already made an extensive collection of early spring plants which grow in this part of the country.

When I arrived at Red River last November, I made arrangements for engaging men who were to proceed, in the beginning of March, 1858, on foot to Carlton; and on my arrival to this place I learned that these men had arrived on the 7th of April, and were afterwards obliged to go out to the south of the Eagle Hills, where they supported themselves by hunting the buffalo, there being no provisions to spare at Carlton.

In the succeeding three years Palliser's expedition worked westward across the prairies and mountains to the Pacific Coast. They made no further use of the Carlton Trail, except that some of their men from the Red River Settlement returned home over it.

PROFESSOR HIND

In the year 1858 Henry Youle Hind, a University of Toronto professor, covered much of Saskatchewan in charge of an exploration party sent out by the Canadian Government. His party crossed southern Manitoba, then turned northwestward to Fort Ellice which it reached on July the ninth. Hind (12) wrote, "Provisions were very scarce at the post, and had it not been for the fortunate arrival of the [fort] hunters with some pemmican and dried meat, we should have been compelled to hunt or kill the ox." The ox had been brought along as emergency provisions.

From Fort Ellice he and his party proceeded up the south side of the Qu'Appelle Valley to the Elbow of the South Saskatchewan River, visiting the mission at Fort Qu'Appelle on the way. On July the thirtieth, at the Elbow, Hind launched a canoe which had been brought by the expedition all the way from the Red River Settlement, and with three companions descended the south branch of the Saskatchewan to its junction

25

with the north branch near Fort à la Corne. This was eight years before Nisbet's group founded the Prince Albert Mission. At Fort à la Corne he secured horses and a half-breed helper and a Cree guide and traveled around the west side of the Birch Hills to a point on the Carlton Trail, near the present site of Wakaw, which he reached on August the twelfth. From this point he followed the Carlton Trail back to Fort Garry. On his way through the Touchwood Hills, Hind wrote a very interesting description of that district and described the location of the first Hudson's Bay post at the Touchwood Hills, at that time in charge of a Mr. Hoover:

In the afternoon we began the ascent of a gently rolling slope at the foot of the Touchwood Hills; patches of willow appear here fringing small areas of good pasturage. At 6:00 p.m. we reached the summit plateau, and then passed through a very beautiful undulating country diversified with many picturesque lakes and aspen groves, possessing land of the best quality, and covered with the most luxuriant herbage. From the west side of the summit plateau, the Quill Lakes are seen to the northwest [actually northeast]; these bodies of water have long been celebrated for the large number of goose quills which were occasionally collected there by Indians, and brought to the fort for exportation. There is no timber visible on the west side of the range with the exception of small aspen and burnt willow bushes. All the wild flowers so numerous and beautiful in the valley of Long Creek are met with on the summit plateau of the Touchwood Hills, of even larger growth and in greater profusion. Little prairie openings fringed with aspen occur here and there, through which the trail passes; we then come suddenly on to the banks of a romantic lakelet, in which ducks with their young broods are swimming, and flocks of white cranes* start from their secluded haunts at so unexpected an intrusion. The breadth of this beautiful plateau is about four miles, its level above the Salt Prairie to the west may be about five hundred feet. Our course lay diagonally across it, so that we had to pass through seven miles of this delightful country. The Heart Hill [Fig. 8], with others not seen before, comes into view as we approach the eastern limit and begin a descent to Touch-

---

*These birds were Whooping Cranes, now nearly extinct.

wood Hills Fort. The Last Mountain is visible in the west [actually southwest], but blue in the distance; the Little Touchwood Hills lie before us, the trail to Fort Ellice stretching toward their eastern flank. The country between the two ranges is dotted with lakes and groves of aspen. From a small hill near the fort I counted forty-seven lakes.

The garden, or rather the remains of a garden in the rear of the fort, produces every variety of vegetable grown in Canada, but the efforts to cultivate it are almost abandoned in consequence of the depredations committed by the Indians from the prairies, when they arrive in autumn with their supplies of provisions [buffalo meat and pemmican]. A few of the lakes near the fort are known to contain fish, and it is probable that all the large fresh water lakes contain them. The officer in temporary charge of the post stated that the people here had only known of the existence of white-fish in the Last Mountain Lake [Fig. 9], for three years; they are now taken in the fall, and it is probable that the fishery

FIG. 8—*A scene in the Big Touchwoods from the top of what Hind called "Heart Hill," or Ka-ou-ta-at-tin-ak.*

27

F<small>IG</small>. 9—*Prairie trail and railroad at south end of Last Mountain Lake.*

recently established will become of great importance to this part
of the country. The Plain Crees are not fisherman like the Ojib-
ways; they did not know how to catch fish when the attention
of the people at the Touchwood Hills Fort was first directed to
the treasures of Last Mountain Lake. Mr. Hoover, the officer in
charge at the time of my visit, told me that he had first observed
the white-fish under the ice in November of 1854, and since that
period they have established a fishery which provides the fort with
an ample supply for winter consumption.

The whole of Hind's report is full of references to buffalo
and Indians (Fig. 10), in the territory over which he traveled.
In this respect it is in marked contrast to that of John Macoun
who explored the same territory about twenty years later, when
the buffalo were practically extinct and the Indians were cooped
up on the newly created Indian reserves.

THE EARL OF SOUTHESK

In 1859 the Earl of Southesk came to the Hudson's Bay
Company's territories for his health and to enjoy the sport of
big game hunting. He sailed from Liverpool on April the

fifteenth on a paddle-wheel steamer and arrived in New York on April the twenty-eighth. After visiting Niagara Falls he went to Lachine, on the St. Lawrence River, where he was welcomed by Sir George Simpson. On May the ninth he set out in company with the latter and several others for the Red River Settlement. They passed the first night in Toronto where the Earl met the artist, Paul Kane. Simpson's party reached St. Paul on May the thirteenth and Fort Garry on June the first where they were received with cheering and a cannon salute in honor of the Governor-in-Chief of the Hudson's Bay Company's Territories.

Here the Earl of Southesk spent some time assembling a party of eight men, mostly of Scottish extraction, and a four-wheeled wagon and three new Red River carts, heavily loaded with a variety of equipment and supplies. Being an ardent sportsman he included an extensive collection of the latest guns. Also there were tents, blankets, and oilcloth squares; sugar, flour, tea, and rice; biscuits, jam, and dried buffalo tongues; and a ninety-pound roll of course twist tobacco to give to any Indians they might meet. They had fifteen horses, including two special buffalo runners.

During the course of their travels they followed the Carlton Trail to Fort Ellice, and then departed from it and followed the Qu'Appelle Valley to the Elbow, crossed the South Saskatchewan about forty miles northwest of the Elbow, traveled past the northwest corner of Goose Lake, and hunted buffalo for a time in the Eagle Hill Creek district. Here the Earl's party met a group of buffalo hunters from Fort Carlton. He made a side trip from their combined camp to the edge of the Missouri Coteau, near the present town of Stranraer, where he shot a grizzly bear. After this they visited Forts Carlton, Pitt, and Edmonton. Then they explored some of the eastern valleys of the Rocky Mountains, going as far south as the Bow River before returning to Edmonton. They had the misfortune to meet

29

with an early winter, so that after boating downstream for a day or so, they were frozen in on October the twentieth. Obtaining horses at Fort Pitt, they proceeded to Carlton with horse sleds on which to carry their baggage. Leaving Carlton on November the nineteenth they traveled over the Carlton Trail to the Touchwood Hills post, which they reached on November the twenty-eighth. Here they branched off on the Fort Pelly Trail. At Fort Pelly they were forced to give up their horses because of the depth of the snow and proceed to Fort Garry by dog train, via the lake posts of western Manitoba, reaching their destination January the eighth, 1860.

Two extracts from the Earl's book (41) will illustrate the conditions under which they traveled the Carlton Trail. The first was written as they approached the Little Saskatchewan River in Manitoba in the month of June; the latter describes their crossing of the Quill Plains and their arrival at Touchwood Hills post about the end of November:

Fig. 10—*Indian encampment on the open prairie.*

McKay had spoken much about the dangerous position of our camp, as lying in the direct war-path of the Sioux, so when morning came and it was reported that Black, Morgan, and Vermont were amissing, I feared that they were lost forever. Happily they had only strayed, and not more than an hour was wasted in tracking and recovering the wanderers.

This was another lovely day, but, for all that, we rejoiced when a thunder-storm came on, for it drove away those pests — the venomous, eye-blinding, hard-skinned little sandflies. Yesterday another enemy had troubled us — certain huge-headed gadflies, of hornet appearance, that are commonly known as "bull-dogs." Darting on man and horse, the wretch gives one short bite with his scissory clippers — then off like a flash, leaving a poisoned and bleeding wound.

The insect tribe is a perfect curse; one has no rest or peace. Mosquitoes on the wet ground and sandflies in the dry; bull-dogs in the sunshine; bugs in the oaklands; ants everywhere — it is maddening . . . . The fever caused by these bites is what most distresses me. It is worst at night, when one gets warm in bed; all the veins swell and glow, and seem full of liquid fire.

After dinner we were detained till three o'clock by another thunder-storm, and then made a four hour's march through a prairie country with numerous small lakes abounding in ducks. I shot a few, but my sport was much interfered with by a dog we had brought with us — a retriever that would not retrieve.

This detestable animal, Hector by name, a large, red, curly-coated water spaniel, I had bought rather hastily from a man at Red River, who gave him a high character, but the dog was an imposter and a nuisance. He would go into the water after a dead or wounded duck, secure it zealously, and bring it with him in the most promising style, but on coming near shore he always dropped it just out of your reach, and no persuasion could make him fetch it an inch further. Sometimes he amused himself by running forward and putting everything up. It was hard to say if he were more knave or fool — and the beast was a coward too.

Sunday, November 27th: Marched for about three hours among brush and poplar clumps, and at noon found ourselves at the edge of a great plain, utterly bare, bounded by a faint blue line of distant wood, amidst which some low hills appeared. McKay and I held a short consultation — whether to camp now, or push on without stopping for dinner, at the risk of having to camp on the open plain, without fuel — and decided on the latter course, as we could not bear losing another day. Accordingly we marched. At sunset the woods appeared little nearer than before, but we pressed on till long after dark, hoping to reach some shelter. Suddenly we found ourselves in a swamp, of the kind that never completely freezes [alkali]; our horses were plunging about up to their girths in mire; it became impossible to proceed, so we halted where we were and took a hasty supper, consisting of cold pemmican, with water we succeeded in melting from snow by burning wisps of grass. If there had been rushes, we might have made a hot enough fire to boil our kettle, but with grass this cannot be done.

The night was not so cold as it often is, and we slept pretty comfortably. The wind was south-west and not high; had a storm arisen, the horses, unable to endure it on so bare a plain, would have run before the wind all night, and we should probably have lost them.

November 28th: Set off about 8 o'clock, with a bitter cold south-easterly gale right in our faces. We crossed the swamp by going round a little way, and hoped to gain the woods, which seemed about six miles distant, but we were woefully deceived, through the levelness of the snow-covered plain, and it cost us three hours and a half of hard work to get to the first poplar clumps, which are several miles from the real woods themselves. Breakfast and fire, however, were so welcome as to remove all discontented feelings; and at two o'clock we continued our march, intending to camp about sunset; but, just as we thought of halting, we came upon fresh snow-shoe tracks, from the very direction in which we supposed the fort to lie—so we went on, in the faint hope of getting there that night [Fig. 11].

The light at this season keeps tolerably good for more than an hour after sunset, and the clearness of the sky enabled us to follow the tracks; it grew very dark at last, and we were preparing to halt, but at that moment heard the barking of dogs, and riding to the brow of the next slope beheld sparks proceeding from a chimney; a welcome illumination, which in a few minutes guided us to the door of Touchwood Hills Fort—where we were hospitably received by the superintendent, Mr. Taylor. It was a great pleasure to find three newspapers with European news up to the thirtieth of June—

Fig. 11—*Tracks of a solitary human crossing the park country in winter.*

the time of the conclusion of the armistice after the battle of Solferino.

November 29th: A tremendous storm set in, with high north-west wind and heavy snow; we were glad to be safely sheltered in the Fort. It was a rough little settlement, but extremely habitable in its way; the large room in particular with its log-piled hearth directly opposite the door, was the very model of homely comfort and cheerfulness.

While there, Mr. Taylor told the Earl of Southesk that according to reports which he had received, the Earl's party barely missed trouble from both Cree and Blackfoot near the Elbow the previous summer, and had been saved by the Indians becoming involved in a skirmish with each other.

Regarding a change of site for the Company's post at the Touchwood Hills the Earl remarked, "I doubt if the fort we then quitted any longer exists, for we heard of an intention to

move it the following summer to Little Touchwood Hills . . ."
This intention was carried out when the second Touchwood
Hills post was built about fourteen miles south of the first site.

THE OVERLANDERS

The lure of gold, to be found in the Cariboo district of
British Columbia, induced several parties of adventurers from
the eastern part of Canada to cross the Prairies from Fort Garry
to Fort Edmonton and to go from there over the mountains in
the year 1859. It is said that three parties, numbering sixty men
in all, followed the Carlton Trail that year, but apparently they
left no written records and little is known of their experiences.
In 1862, however, they were followed by several parties among
whom were a number who possessed a penchant for keeping
diaries (45). Thanks to them we know something definite
about the doings of these later overland travelers. In the first
party there were about 150 men organized into eight "battil-
lions." Certain rather interesting rules were adopted as to the
duties and conduct of the men. Among other things it was agreed
that Thos. McMicking was to be captain of the whole party
and that he was to be assisted by a committee composed of
one representative from each group. He was to determine the
hours of travel, the camping arrangements, and the order of
precedence in the line of march, and he was also to direct the
guide. The guide was to be their only mouthpiece in case they
came into contact with any Indians, and no one was to trade with
the Indians for fear of starting disputes with the aborigines.
No liquor was to be used among the natives. The men took
their turns at cooking, sentry duty, and all other necessary
chores.

They started out from Fort Garry on June the fifth and
on the evening of June the twelfth camped at Shoal Lake.
At this place, according to a diary kept by a Mr. Seller:

After supper some went fishing, some shooting, while many others were amusing themselves playing on different kinds of brass instruments, claranetts, fluits, violins, etc., and a concertena, and some two or three groups were gathered together singing over a few favorite pieces of vocal music which wiled away the hours of the evening till bed time.

When they reached the Assiniboine River they found a rude scow on which they ferried all their oxen and carts across the river in small installments. Thos. McMicking wrote of the factor then in charge of Fort Ellice:

Mr. McKay, the master of the fort is an obliging gentleman, and, in common with the rest of his countrymen, keeps a prudent eye to business and a sharp look-out after the bawbees.

They stayed over Sunday at Fort Ellice and the Rev. Mr. Settee, a native missionary, preached a sermon in the fort which was attended by many of the McMicking party.

Apparently the prospective miners were not all equally adaptable to pioneering activities. Seller's diary contains this entry as evidence of the fact: "There we together split off from the main body and travelled ahead, the cause being the delay of certain parties who know nothing about carts and cattle or anything else save standing and looking at others working, or getting behind a counter, neither of which will be of any benefit to a man when his ox and cart is stuck fast in a mudhole."

It is stated that on June the twenty-fourth they entered the Touchwood Hills and passed the old deserted fort. This was situated about six miles north and two miles west of the present town of Punnichy. In 1861 a new post had been built about fourteen miles south, near an Indian Mission on the western edge of the Little Touchwood Hills. The Overlanders gathered their first wild strawberries near the deserted post.

After crossing the Quill Plains, they passed through a magnificent country of alternate woodland and prairie where the grass grew luxuriantly in the open spaces. From the number of buffalo bones and old buffalo trails and wallows which they saw they concluded that this was one of the favorite hunting grounds of the Indians and Métis.

On June the thirtieth they reached the South Saskatchewan River at Batoche. There they found a large batteau, the property of the Hudson's Bay Company, on which they were able to ferry six carts and their loads at each trip. The cattle and horses were forced into the river and made to swim across it. In the excitement of driving the livestock into the river, one of the men got into deep water and was nearly drowned. Expert swimmers pulled him out of the water and brought him back through the gates of death by means of artificial respiration.

On July the first they arrived at Fort Carlton, having traveled the five hundred and some odd miles from Fort Garry in twenty-five days. The Fort at that time was in charge of a Mr. Lillie. It is stated that 300 Indian hunters and trappers were attached to this post, largely for the purpose of bringing in pemmican to supply the servants of the Hudson's Bay Company throughout the north country. Here the Overlanders had their first taste of buffalo meat, as they were able to purchase some in the fresh state at the post. They were very glad of the change and found that the meat resembled beef, but it was a little coarser in the grain and more juicy. The Overlanders wasted no time here but ferried their equipment over the north branch at once and proceeded westward.

MILTON AND CHEADLE

The next characters to roll across our stage were, of all things, tourists! A couple of adventurous Englishmen, Dr. Cheadle and Lord Milton, decided to cross Rupert's Land on horseback just for the interest and excitement of the trip. Accordingly they set out from Fort Garry on August the twenty-third, 1862, with a traveling companion named Messiter, and several half-breed servants and Red River carts, to carry their "impedimenta." They arrived at Fort Carlton on September the twenty-six, so they did not get over the trail as rapidly as did the Overlanders.

At Fort Ellice, Lord Milton purchased an Indian lodge made of buffalo skins. It was "nicely" painted on the outside with scenes depicting Indian warfare. It was obtained by bartering for it a plated calumet, and a cart cover to protect the Indian's family until he could make a new lodge. The tourists used this skin lodge as a tent throughout much of their subsequent journey.

As they traveled along they shot enough ducks and prairie chickens to supply most of their food.

The following excerpts from Dr. Cheadle's diary (3) mention camping near the site of the first Hudson's Bay post

FIG. 12—*Doctor Cheadle's "miniature Derwentwater" as it appeared in July, 1949. The "wooded island" is on the right. From all appearances this lakelet was once fifteen to eighteen feet deep.*

in the Touchwood Hills, and describe their crossing of the South Saskatchewan and their arrival at Fort Carlton:

Thursday, September 18th: At sundown came upon Touchwood Hills. Old fort; pretty situation, rounded hills, etc. Autumn tints at sunset very fine. Encamp just beyond fort near pretty lake with round wooded island in centre very like a miniature Derwentwater. [Fig. 12]. . . .

Thursday, September 25th: Through wooded country with numerous lakes and arrive at South Saskatchewan at noon. Camp on bank, dine. After dinner men cut down trees, make raft, and cross for Company's barge; unload carts, and transfer all baggage and selves to the other bank, leaving carts and horses behind to be fetched in the morning. Saskatchewan about eighty yards wide here, muddy stream, wooded banks, muddy and stony at edges. Make Canada fire in road under trees and sleep in open air.

Friday, September 26th: In early morning carts taken to pieces and brought across in barge. The horses driven in and swam across, causing some trouble and enduring severe lodge-polling before they could be induced to enter the water. I contradict Messiter in the same manner he uses to others, and he becomes very irate. We don't speak for some time. I walk on ten or twelve miles and the carts come up. I get my horse and stay behind to lunch on pemmican with Milton. I find that he and Messiter have had a violent quarrel about nothing and nearly come to blows. We agree that it will be better to separate, as his cross-grained temper will be monotonous during six months of winter. Milton does not like to mention it and pities him more than I do; left open. Milton's horse meanwhile breaks away and I lend him mine to go for him; catches him at last, and brings back mine. We canter forward five or six miles and suddenly come into a broad track and after about a half mile of this see the fort in the valley below close to the river. Carts descending by another route. Find Mr. Lillie at Fort very civil and invites us to tea. Fresh buffalo meat for the first time; steaks very good. Delighted with news that buffalo bulls are within half a day, the cows two days. Resolve to stay next day and Sunday and prepare, commence campaign on Monday. Lodge erected near river close to Fort. No Indians here except few old ones; rest after buffalo. Blackfeet not near except in spring. Snow comes on.

Saturday, September 27th: Have famous sleep. The Company's

jealousy of other traders. Mr. Lillie sends for La Ronde and pumps him about our rum and goods. Snow fallen some four inches during the night and still continues (12 noon). Send to Fort for potatoes, milk and marrow fat, and have famous breakfast. Make what preparations we can but unable to get boxes on account of snow, not daring to uncover the carts. Very slow day. Fort better than Ellis [sic]; high pallisade with platform, round and square towers at corners. North Saskatchewan very similar to South. Messiter very agreeable. Snow continued all day; in evening went to Fort and got some sulphur for our itch; bought three pairs moccasins (buffalo) 1s. per pair. Wretched old Cree with liver disease asks for rum; not got any.

Sunday, September 28th: A very raw cold thaw; cleaned gun, patched bulb, and separated things for this hunt, sending the rest to the Fort until our return. In afternoon went to the Fort and prepared sulphur ointment. Invited to tea with Mr. Lillie who gave us stewed buffalo steaks; very good indeed. Milton made cartridges in the evening. Delighted with the news that 2 grisly bears were seen about 5 miles from the Fort. Mr. Lillie very kindly promised to keep the man [Peter the interpreter] who had seen them, to take us to the place at daybreak next morning. Peter had discovered the tracks whilst bringing in the horses to the Fort that evening; followed them and discovered two full grown grislys tearing up roots; stated he dismounted, loaded his gun and prepared to shoot at them when he suddenly remembered it was Sunday. La Ronde for some reason or other set himself against hunting the bears, thought he would not find them in the morning, etc., etc.; went to bed rather late, giving instructions to be called at daybreak.

Our ardent hunters were unable to find the grizzly bears, which was perhaps just as well for all concerned, but a few days later they did succeed in finding and shooting buffalo in the district along the Eagle Hill Creek west of where Saskatoon now stands. After that they returned to Carlton and then went out to a point somewhere west of the present site of the town of Leask where they built a log cabin with the help of a half-breed servant. There they spent the winter and during the following spring and summer they proceeded on to Edmonton and over the Rockies to the Pacific Coast in 1863.

THE McDOUGALLS—MISSIONARIES TO THE INDIANS

We will now turn our attention to two men who settled in the Saskatchewan country and who by their arduous and faithful labors as Christian missionaries, left an indelible impression on the people and history of this new land. These two were George McDougall and his son John. Coming into the country in 1862, they established a Wesleyan Methodist mission at a point about seventy miles down the North Saskatchewan River from Edmonton. They named this place Victoria. Subsequently they established two other missions, one at Edmonton and another at Morleyville on the Bow River. They traveled far and wide in their attempts to Christianize the Indians and prepare them for the great changes to come when the white people would move in and settle the Prairies. They made repeated trips to the buffalo feeding grounds for supplies of meat and took part in many exciting hunts with the half-breeds and Indians. They also made many trips over the Carlton Trail, accounts of which are to be found in the series of books written by John McDougall in later years. The father perished after becoming lost in the foothill country in January, 1876. The influence of their teaching helped greatly in keeping many of the Indians from going on the warpath in sympathy with the Métis in 1870 and in 1885.

Coming from Ontario in 1860, the McDougall family spent two years at the Indian mission near Norway House at the north end of Lake Winnipeg. In 1862 John came up the Saskatchewan River with a brigade of York boats bringing supplies to the Hudson's Bay posts along the north branch of that great river. At the same time his father went down to Fort Garry by boat and then came in over the Carlton Trail on horseback. After the first year or so at the new mission they had to bring in their own supplies, so in the spring of 1864, John was sent to Fort Garry with an Indian helper to bring in the necessary supplies by Red River cart. They traveled in company with several others from another mission. On the way down he and his companions shot several antelope in the Wakaw district and killed a bear in the Touchwood Hills, which together with game birds and birds' eggs, gave some variety to their diet. They also fell in with a brigade of Métis traders from Lac la Biche, with whom they traveled in friendly company for a time before pressing on ahead. Let John describe his experiences, near Fort Ellice, in his own words (25):

Continuing our journey, we left these people to come on more slowly. We crossed Pheasant Plains and Cut Arm Creek and camped one evening on the high bank of the Qu'Appelle River [Fig. 13], beside a spring. In the evening shade, as we were sitting beside our camp-fire, suddenly I heard a cry which thrilled through my whole being; "Whip-poor-will-Whip-poor-will!" came echoing through the woods and up the valley, and in a moment I was among the scenes of my childhood paddling a birch canoe along the shores of the Great Lakes, rioting among the beech and maple

FIG. 13—*Looking north across the Qu'Appelle Valley at the upper end of Katepwa Lake.*

woods of old Ontario. For years I had not heard the whip-poor-will and now the once familiar sounds brought with them a feeling of home-sickness.

"The next afternoon Ka-Kake and I, leaving our companions to cross the Assiniboine above the mouth of the Qu'Appelle, detoured by way of Fort Ellice, and here also I had a memorable experience. Mrs. MacKay [sic], the wife of the gentleman in charge of the fort, very kindly invited me to have supper with them. As we would have plenty of time to rejoin our party afterwards, I gladly accepted, and what should be on the table but pancakes and maple syrup! I had not even tasted anything cooked from flour for some time. I had not tasted maple syrup for four years and had not had a slice of bread for two years. No wonder I can never forget those cakes and syrup! Verily the memory of them is still sweet to my taste. Not that I am an epicure—by no means—but these were things I had been accustomed to, almost bred on, all my life previous to coming to the North-West.

A few days later they passed a large band of Métis hunters, from the Red River Settlement, starting out on the summer hunt with about 500 carts. When John and his companion came to the White Mud River they found the Rev. Mr. George in charge of an Anglican mission there. John wrote, "Mrs. George was very kind, and for the first time in two years I had a square meal of bread and butter. Oh! How good it was." The next morning, as they started on their way, Mrs. George gave them a fresh loaf and some butter for their noonday lunch. However, they were barely out of sight of the home of their kind hostess when they dismounted and fell upon the bread and butter and ate them to the last crumb with eager relish!

Arriving at Fort Garry, John secured supplies for the mission and carts and oxen with which to transport the goods. He also bought four milch cows. The oxen cost about thirty-five dollars apiece and the cows cost about half that much. The flour cost about eight dollars per hundred pounds. He also saw "Hudson's Bay blankets" for the first time. These were large five-shilling and five-pound notes, issued by the Company.

After conducting his business and visiting some friends he commenced the long return journey with a Mr. Connor and his son for additional company. On the way back an Indian attempted to steal their horses somewhere in the Humboldt district, and John's account of the affair makes interesting reading:

I think it was the fourth day afterwards [after meeting Indians in the Touchwood Hills] that we camped in a small round prairie, backed by a range of hills and fringed around by willow and poplar bush. We had pulled our carts into a line, with our camp-fire in the middle. We were sufficiently north, as we thought, to be comparatively free from horse-thieves and war parties, so we merely hobbled our horses, and making a good smudge near our own fire, we rolled in our blankets, each man under a cart, except for Mr. Connor who slept in his. Some time in the night I was awakened by my little dog, who had crept under my blanket as usual, and now startled me by springing forth and barking vigorously. As I raised myself on elbow, I saw that the two larger dogs were charging at something quite near. The moon was about three parts full, and the night quiet and almost clear. From under the shadow of the cart I could see our horses feeding near the smoke [of the smudge]. Presently I discovered an object crawling up to come between the carts and the horses. At first I thought it was a big grey wolf, but as the dogs rushed at it, I saw that it did not recede, but came on. I reached for my gun and watched closely, and presently saw the object pick up a stick and throw it at the dogs. This convinced me that it was someone trying to steal our horses. His object evidently was to creep in between us and our stock, and gently driving them away, he would then cut off the hobbles and run them off.

Having made sure that what I saw was a human being, and a would-be-horse-thief, or worse, I immediately planned to intercept him. So I in turn began to crawl along the shade of the carts until I was under the last one, which was Mr. Connor's. Here I waited and watched until, seeing the fellow repeatedly frighten the dogs away, I was sure it was a man. He was slowly coming up on hands and knees, and now near the first horse, when I took deliberate aim and fired at him. My gun was loaded with shot and fortunately for him was only a single barrel, or I would have given him the other,

43

for I was not at that moment in a mood to spare a horse-thief. My shot at once knocked him down flat. When the smoke had cleared away I saw him starting to crawl off, so I jumped for him, on which he rose to his feet and ran for all he was worth towards the nearest bush. I dropped my gun and picked up a pole that lay in my way, and was over-taking him fast when he reached the thicket; then thinking he might not be alone, I ran back for my gun. My companions by this time were all up, and we made ready for an attack. Tying up our horses we watched and guarded until daylight, but were not further molested.

One can imagine the fright Mr. Connor got when John's gun went off right under his cart! Horse thieves certainly took their lives in their hands in those days.

On reaching the South Saskatchewan they found the river in full flood and they had a terribly difficult and dangerous task to get their carts and livestock across. Finally they accomplished this without loss of either life or property, but it was "touch and go" for a time. As if this were not trouble enough their horses strayed away shortly after they got over the river. John's feet

Fig. 14—*A minor trail in the park country covered by a blanket of snow in early winter. Trees and shrubs bear a glistening coat of hoar frost.*

were badly cut from the labors of ferrying their things over the river but he set out to look for the lost animals, and after hours of painful and painstaking tracking, they were finally found and galloped back to camp in disgrace. The travelers were then able to continue their journey and succeeded in crossing the North Saskatchewan at Carlton the next day with much less anxiety and effort.

The McDougalls made several other trips over the Carlton Trail to secure provisions for their missions, or to bring in relatives and missionary helpers from Eastern Canada. In 1872, father and son traveled down to Winnipeg together to attend a conference of Methodist church and mission officials (28). At this conference John was ordained. While there, they met Sandford Fleming and his party. After the conference was over, George McDougall returned to the Saskatchewan country with the Fleming party. John proceeded to Ontario where he married his second wife. On their arrival at Fort Garry, on the return trip, he was unable to find anyone to make the trip with them to Edmonton because it was so late in the season. So, with his young wife driving a "democrat," and he on horseback driving a cart and several loose horses, they made a lonely trip to Carlton through the snow storms of an early winter (Fig. 14). Among the few people they saw on this 500-mile stretch were a party of Sioux Indians and some Hudson's Bay officials, including Factor McDonald of Fort Qu'Appelle and Factor McMurray, who was then stationed in the Athabaska River country. During the latter part of their trip they ran into blizzards and deep snow between Carlton and Victoria but they finally arrived at their destination safely.

A DOG TEAM ON THE CARLTON TRAIL

Going back for a moment to March, 1867, I should like to mention a trip by dog team over the Carlton Trail. It was made by a small party of Catholic missionaries and their dog drivers.

45

Father Lacombe came down from the prairie south of Edmonton to meet Bishop Grandin at Carlton (13). The latter was returning from a tour of inspection of the missions to the northwest. On the way from Fort Pitt to Carlton, Father Lacombe was stricken with snow blindness. After a terrible trip, he arrived at Carlton only to find that the Bishop had given up hopes of seeing him and had started down the Carlton Trail for St. Boniface earlier in the day. However, Father Lacombe was determined not to miss seeing the Bishop, so he immediately started out after him without even stopping to rest his weary dogs (both human and canine) and the hardy priest finally reached the Bishop's camp on the South Saskatchewan River long after midnight. From this camp the Bishop persuaded Father Lacombe to accompany him to St. Boniface, so they started off next morning with the priest tucked away in the cariole and the Bishop running behind on snowshoes. It is recorded that Father Lacombe was so exhausted from the exertions of the previous few days that he fell asleep in the cariole and never awoke until the evening camp was reached. However, by the following morning he was fresh again and ready to change places with the Bishop for the remainder of the journey.

THE REV. JAMES NISBET

In 1866 the Presbyterian Church established an Indian mission at a point on the North Saskatchewan River about sixty miles below Fort Carlton (23). The first missionary sent to this place was the Rev. James Nisbet and he called the place Prince Albert in honor of the Prince Consort. This seemed fitting, as the Methodist mission higher up the river near Edmonton was called Victoria.

James Nisbet and his party of helpers, with their wives and several children, came into the Saskatchewan country over the Carlton Trail. Their caravan consisted of eleven carts and a light wagon. They left Kildonan on June the sixth, 1866, and reached Carlton about the middle of July. Here he was joined by Mr. George Flett. Leaving most of the party at Carlton for about a week, he and Mr. Flett searched out a suitable site for the new mission and obtained permission from the Cree Indians to occupy it. Then the whole party floated down the river on a raft to their new home in the wilderness.

There is very little firsthand information about their trip over the trail from Kildonan to Carlton, but the following is an excerpt from one of James Nisbet's letters:

All our goods were carried in carts; each cart was drawn by one ox, harnessed something like a horse. Mrs. Nisbet and our little girl and a young woman rode on a light wagon with a canvas top, such as you sometimes use in Canada. For myself I was generally on horseback but frequently walking, as the oxen do not go very fast. We had tents, such as soldiers use, which we pitched every night, and in them we were generally very comfortable. The Sabbaths were delightful to us. Both men and animals were prepared for the weekly rest. It was pleasant to see the poor oxen evidently enjoying the rich pasture of the wilderness and the rest they had from their daily toil. We had regular Sabbath services, and they were very devout.

We had a good many creeks and rivers to cross, and I dare say you would have been much amused, had you seen the plans that were fallen upon for crossing such as were too deep for loaded carts. Few of my friends in the east have seen a boat made with two cartwheels tied together and an oilcloth spread over them, or one made of ox-hides sewed together and stretched on a rough frame, that would take two carts and their loads at a time. Such were the contrivances for getting over streams where there are no bridges or large boats by which we could cross. We passed over a great deal of beautiful country, with hills and valleys, streams, lakes, and ponds. Hundreds of ducks were swimming about in the little lakes, and sometimes they furnished dinners for us. Sandhill cranes were also seen occasionally, and a few of them were shot for our Sabbath dinners. Forty days after we left our Red River homes we got to a place called Carlton House, on the north branch of the great Saskatchewan River, and there we camped for one week, while I went to see some places that I could fix upon for our future home.

This was the beginning of the Prince Albert settlement, the first agricultural one in the area now included in the province of Saskatchewan. Pioneer farmers began to occupy the district surrounding the mission about 1873. From that year on, the population of the settlement continued to grow, and increased use was made of the Carlton Trail for the purpose of bringing in new settlers, and for freighting in supplies for those already established there. A new branch of the Trail was made from the west bank of the river at Batoche to the new mission. In later years a different route was developed. This led south and crossed the river near St. Louis and joined the old trail near Wakaw.

CAPTAIN BUTLER

In the late autumn of 1870, a colorful figure, in the person of Captain W. F. Butler, traveled the Carlton Trail on a peculiar mission. Captain Butler had come out from England as a free lance to have a part in suppressing the Red River Rebellion. In October he left Fort Garry with a Hudson's Bay Company's officer and a French half-breed as companions. He was commissioned by Governor Archibald to confer the office of "justice of the peace" upon two residents of the Saskatchewan country and also to take supplies of smallpox vaccine and instructions relating to smallpox and its control to any Hudson's Bay factors and missionaries that he could visit. The reason for this latter assignment was the terrible epidemic which had swept the Saskatchewan region the previous summer. He was also to bring back a report as to the condition of the various Indian tribes and small settlements of whites and Métis, as intercourse between them and the Red River Settlement had been forbidden during the epidemic.

Captain Butler's party left Fort Garry on October the twenty-fourth and arrived at Fort Carlton on November the eighth. The only record we have of a faster trip over the Trail is that of Sir George Simpson and his party in 1841. Butler and his companions had a Red River cart, a buckboard, and seven horses. Here are a few extracts from his story of the trip (2):

The days that now commenced to pass were filled from dawn to dark with unceasing travel; clear, bright days of mellow sunshine followed by nights of sharp frost which almost imperceptibly made stronger the icy covering of the pools and carried farther and farther out into the running streams the edging of ice which so soon was destined to cover completely the river and the rill. Our route lay along the left bank of the Assiniboine, but at a considerable distance from the river, whose winding course could be marked at times by the dark oak woods that fringed it. Far away to the south rose the outline of the Blue Hills of the Souris, and to the north the Riding Mountains lay faintly upon the horizon.

As they approached Fort Ellice they passed a Métis trader, with a number of horses hauling carts filled with merchandise, on his way to the Missouri Coteau to trade with the Sioux. To quote again, Butler wrote:

I remained only long enough at Fort Ellice to complete a few changes in costume which the rapidly increasing cold made necessary. Boots and hat were finally discarded, the stirrup-irons were rolled in strips of buffalo skin, the large moose-skin "mittaines" taken into wear, and immense moccasins got ready. These precautions were necessary, for before us there now lay a great open region with treeless expanses that were sixty miles across them—a vast tract of rolling hill and plain over which, for three hundred miles, there lay no fort or house of any kind.

About midway between Fort Ellice and Carlton a sudden well-defined change occurs in the character of the country; the light soil disappears, and its place is succeeded by a rich dark loam covered deep in grass and vetches. Beautiful hills swell in slopes more or less abrupt on all sides, while lakes fringed with thickets and clumps of good-sized poplar balsam lie lapped in their fertile hollows.

This region bears the name of the Touchwood Hills. Around it, far into endless space, stretch immense plains of bare and scanty vegetation, plains seared with the tracks of countless buffalo which, until a few years ago, were wont to roam in vast herds between the Assiniboine and the Saskatchewan. Upon whatever side the eye turns when crossing these great expanses the same wrecks of the monarch of the prairie lie thickly strewn over the surface. Hundreds of thousands of skeletons dot the short, scant grass; and when fire has laid barer still the level surface, the bleached ribs and skulls of long-killed bison whiten far and near the dark burnt prairie. There is something unspeakably melancholy in the aspect of this portion of the North-West.

They were forced to make one of their camps in the middle of the Quill Plains beside a small willow bluff. During the night a snowstorm came on and the Hudson's Bay man came near being lost the next morning while hunting their horses, which had strayed away from the camp in the storm. On the night of November the sixth they camped near the Minitchinass (Solitary Hill), about sixteen miles southeast of Batoche, called "Lumpy Hill of the Woods," by Professor Hind.

Arriving at the river they found it frozen except for an open channel down the middle. Being nearly out of provisions and anxious to reach Carlton, they attempted to cross by putting an oilcloth around their light wagon box and sliding it out to thin ice and chopping a channel for it from thence to the open water. However, the oilcloth leaked and it was difficult to cut their way in to solid ice on the far side of the open water and finally the long leather tow-rope broke, so they hadn't made much progress when the second night fell. The third day they found the river frozen right across and after testing it cautiously, they led the first horse across safely. At the next trip, however, Captain Butler's favorite horse, "Blackie," broke through into deep water and had to be shot to put him out of misery, as they could not rescue him. This broke Captain Butler's heart, and he sat down and cried like a child, for he was strongly attached to the faithful animal.

Giving up the attempt to cross the rest of the horses until the ice became stronger, he and the Hudson's Bay man took the one horse and started on to Carlton, leaving a half-breed to guard the others:

From the high north bank I took one last look back at the South Saskatchewan—it lay in its broad deep valley glittering in one great band of purest snow; but I loathed the sight of it, while the small round hole, dwarfed to a speck by distance, marked the spot where my poor horse had found his grave, after having carried me so faithfully through the long, lonely wilds.

On arriving at Carlton they learned that the smallpox epidemic was over, but before it had run its course thirty-two out of about sixty who lived around the place had died! The list of dead included the former officer in charge of the fort. To add to the depression which had settled about the fort, provisions were scarce because of the difficulty of reaching the buffalo which were far out on the plains.

After leaving Carlton, Captain Butler visited a number of posts and Indian camps to the west, including Battleford, Pitt, Edmonton, and Rocky Mountain House. He reached the last-named place early in December and spent eight days there, part of the time in the company of Father Lacombe. He commenced his return on December the twelfth and reached Victoria on the twenty-second. Here he spent Christmas. He stopped for some time at Fort Pitt to obtain fresh dogs, as he was traveling now by dog team. He returned to Carlton on January the twelfth and that night the temperature went down to twenty below zero in his bedroom at the fort—outside it was about fifty degrees below zero.

Instead of returning to Fort Garry across the Prairies, he followed the Saskatchewan River and Lakes Winnipegosis and Manitoba. Therefore we will say no more of his experiences but turn to others who used the Carlton Trail in subsequent years.

SANDFORD FLEMING

Sandford Fleming was engineer-in-charge of the projected Canadian Pacific Railway, and he crossed the continent in the summer of 1872 to see the country over which the railway was to be built. He had with him the Rev. George M. Grant as his secretary, John Macoun as botanist of the expedition, and three other men besides the guide and helpers necessary to look after the carts, buckboards, and horses. Incidentally, this is one of the first references to a buckboard being used on the Carlton Trail, although Captain Butler and the McDougalls had already used this type of vehicle. Mr. Grant kept a diary of the long journey and we will draw on it for pictures of their experiences (9):

Our first evening on the prairie was like many another which followed it. The sky was a clear, soft, unflecked blue, save all around the horizon, where pure white clouds of many shapes and masses bordered it, like a great shield of which only the rim is embossed. The air was singularly exhilarating, yet sweet and warm, as in more southern latitudes. The road was only the trail made by the ordinary traffic, but it formed nevertheless an excellent carriage road. Far away stretched the level prairie, dotted with islets of aspens; and the sun, in his going down, dipped beneath it as he does beneath the sea. Soon after sunset, we reached our camping place for the night, an open spot on the banks of the river thirty-three miles from Fort Garry, on the east side of Long Lake, with plenty of dry wood for our fires, and good feed for the horses near at hand. Scarcely were our fires lighted when another traveller drove up, the Rev. Mr. McDougall, Wesleyan missionary at Fort Victoria near Edmonton. We cordially welcomed him to our camp, and asked him to join our party. He was well known to us by reputation as a faithful minister, and an intelligent observer of Indian character. He had been nine times over the plains, and evidently knew the country better than our guides. On this occasion, he was accompanied only by his Cree servant Souzie, which being interpreted is Joseph . . .

At four p.m. we started for the next post, Rat Creek, ten miles off. The sky was threatening, but, as we always disregarded appearances, no one proposed a halt. On the open prairie, when just well away from the Hudson Bay Company's store, we saw that we were in for a storm. Every form of beauty was combined in the sky at this time. To the south it was such blue as Titian loved to paint; blue, that those who have seen only dull English skies say is nowhere to be seen but on canvas or in heaven; and the blue was bordered to the west with vast billowy mountains of the fleeciest white. Next to these and right ahead of us and overhead, was a

52

FIG. 15—*Lakelet, with steep wooded shores, in the district east of Cudworth through which the Carlton Trail passed.*

swollen black cloud, along the under surface of which greyer masses were eddying at a terrific rate. Extending from this, and all around the north and east, the expanse was a dun-colored mass livid with lightning, and there, to the right, and behind us, torrents of rain were pouring, and nearing us every minute. The atmosphere was charged with electricity on all sides, lightning rushed towards the earth in straight and zig-zag currents, and the thunder varied from the sharp rattle of musketry to the roar of artillery; still there was no rain and but little wind. We pressed on for a house, not far away; but there was to be no escape. With the suddenness of a tornado the wind struck us, at first without rain—but so fierce that the horses were forced again and again off the track. And now, with the wind came the rain—thick and furious, and then hail— hail mixed with angular lumps of ice from half an inch to an inch across, a blow on the head from one of which was stunning. Our long line of horses and carts was broken. Some of the poor creatures clung to the road, fighting desperately; others were driven into the prairie and, turning their backs to the storm, stood still or moved sideways with cowering heads, their manes and long tails floating wildly like those of the Highland shelties. It was a picture for

53

Rosa Bonheur; the storm driving over the vast prairie, and the men and horses yielding to or fighting against it. In half an hour we got under the shelter of the log house a mile distant; but the fury of the storm was past, and in less than an hour the sun burst forth again, scattering the clouds, till not a blot was left in the sky, save fragments of the mist to the south and east. . . .

At four p.m., we prepared to follow our party, but at this moment a body of sixty or eighty Sioux, noble looking fellows, came sweeping across the prairie in all the glory of paint, feathers, and Indian warlike magnificence. They had come from Fort Ellice, had recently travelled the long road from the Missouri, and were now on their way to Governor Archibald to ask permission to live under the British flag, and that small reserves or allotments of land should be allowed them, as they were determined to live no longer under the rule of "the long knives." Some of them rode horses, others were in light baggage-carts or on foot. All had guns and adornment of one kind or another. A handsome brave came first, with a painted tin horse a foot long hanging from his neck down on his naked brawny breast, skunk fur around his ankles, hawk's feathers on his head, and a great bunch of sweet-smelling lilac bergamot flowers on one arm. An Indian brave has the vanity of a child. We went forward to address him, when he pointed to another as O-ghe-ma (or chief); and, as the band halted, the O-ghe-ma then came up with the usual "Ho, Ho; B'jou, B'jou," and shook hands all around with a dignity of manner that whites in the new world must despair of ever attaining. His distinction was a necklace of bears' claws, and moccasins belted with broad stripes of porcupines' quills dyed a bright gold. Next to him came the medicine man, six feet three inches in height, gaunt and wasted in appearance, with only a single blanket to cover his nakedness. They would have liked a long pow wow, but we had time only for hasty greetings and a few kindly words with them . . .

August 7th—Made a good day's journey of forty-five miles, from the Salt Lake to the junction of the Qu'Appelle and Assiniboine Rivers. The first stage was ten miles, to the Shoal Lake—a large and beautiful sheet of water with pebbly or sandy beach—a capital place for a halt or for camping. The great requirements of such spots are wood, water, and feed for the horses; the traveller has to make his stages square with the absence or presence of these essentials. If he can get a hilly spot where there are few mosquitoes, and a sheet of water large enough to bathe in [Fig. 15] and a resort of game, so much the better. Arrived at the ground, the grassiest and most level spots, gently sloping, if possible, that the head may be higher than the feet, are selected. The tents are pitched over these, one tent being allotted to two persons, when comfort is desirable, though sometimes a dozen crowd inside of one. A waterproof is spread on the ground, and, over that, a blanket. Each man has another blanket to pull over him, and he may be sound asleep within minutes after arriving at the ground, if he has not to cook or wait for his supper. The horses need very little attention, the harness is taken off and they are turned loose—the leaders or most turbulent ones being hobbled, i.e. their fore feet are fettered with intertwined folds of shagannappi or raw buffalo hide, so that they can only move about by a succession of short jumps. Hobbling is the western substitute for tethering. They find out, or are driven to water, and, immediately after drinking begin grazing around; next morning they are ready for the road . . .

August 8th—Being in the neighborhood of a fort, and having to rearrange luggage and look after the new horses, we did not get away till nine o'clock. An hour before, greatly to the surprise of Emilien, who had calculated on keeping in advance the twenty-two miles he had gained on Sunday, and greatly to our delight, Mr. McDougall drove up and rejoined us with his man Souzie. Souzie had never been east before, and the glories of Winnipeg had fairly dazzled him. He was going home heavy laden with wonderful stories of all he had seen—the crowd hearing Mr. Punshon preach and the collection taken up at the close, the review of the battalion of militia, the splendour of the village stores, the Red River steamboat, the quantities of rum, were all amazing. When the plate came round at the church Souzie rejoiced, and was going to help himself, but noticing his neighbors put money in, he was so puzzled that he let it pass . . .

Our next stage was twenty-two miles to Broken Arm River—a pretty little stream with the usual deep and broad valley. The soil improved as we travelled west. The grass was richer, and much of the flora that had disappeared for the previous twenty miles began to show again. On the banks of the river there was time before tea to indulge in a great feast of raspberries, as we camped early this evening, after having travelled only thirty-one miles. The botanist, John Macoun, had found exactly that number of new species—the

55

FIG. 16—*A view of the countryside east of the Little Touchwood Hills as seen from a point about seven miles south of Lestock. "The low line of the Touchwood Hills" shows very faintly in the center of the picture.*

largest number by far on any one day since leaving Fort Garry. The explanation is, that he had botanized over the valleys of two rivers and several varieties of soil . . . .

The low line of the Touchwood Hills had been visible in the forenoon [Fig. 16], and, for the rest of the day's journey, we first skirted them in a north-westerly direction and then turning directly west, we gained the height by a road so winding and an ascent so easy, that there was no point at which we could look back and get an extended view of the ground travelled in the course of the afternoon. It is almost inaccurate to call this section of country by the name of "Hills," little or big. It is simply a series of prairie uplands, from fifty to eighty miles wide, that swell up in beautiful undulations from the level prairies on each side. They have no decided summits from which the ascent and the plain beyond can be seen; but everywhere are grassy or wooded rounded knolls, enclosing fields with small ponds in the windings, and larger ones in the lowest hollows. The land everywhere is of the richest loam. Every acre that we saw might be ploughed. Though not as well suited for steam ploughs as the open prairie, in many respects this section is better adapted for farming purposes, being well wooded, well watered, and with excellent natural drainage, not to speak of its wonderful beauty. All that it lacks is a murmuring brook or brawling burn; but there is not one, partly because the trail is along the watershed. On a parallel road farther north passing by Quill Lake, Mr. McDougall says that there are running streams, and that the country is, of course, all the more beautiful . . .

August 14th — Our first "spell" today was fifteen, and our second twenty miles to "the Round Hill,"* over rolling or slightly broken prairie; the loam was not so rich as usual and had a sandy subsoil. Ridges and hillocks of gravel intersected or broke the general level, so that, should the railway come in this direction, abundant material for ballasting can be promised . . . .

The hill at the foot of which we camped rose abruptly from the rest, like the site of an ancient fortalice. Horetski [sic] described it as a New Zealand pah; one hill, like a wall, enclosing another in its centre, and a deep precipitous valley that would have served admirably as a moat, filled with thick wood and underbrush, between the two. Climbing to the summit of the central hill, we found ourselves in the middle of a circle, thirty to forty miles in diameter, enclosing about a thousand square miles of beautiful country. North and east it was undulating, studded with aspen groves and shining with lakes [Fig. 17]. To the south and west was a level prairie, with a skyline of hills to the south-west. To the north-west — our direction — a prairie fire, kindled probably by embers that had been left carelessly behind at a camp, partly hid the view. Masses of fiery smoke rose from the burning grass and willows, and if there had been a strong wind, or the grass less green and damp, the beauty of much of the fair scene we were gazing on would soon have vanished, and a vast blackened surface alone been left . . . .

August 15th — We met or passed a great many teams and brigades today; traders going west, and half-breeds returning east with carts well laden with buffalo skins and dried meat [Fig. 18]. A number of Red River people club together in the spring and go west to hunt buffalo. Their united caravan is popularly called a brigade, and very picturesque is its appearance on the road or round the campfire. The old men, the women, and little children are engaged

---

* This is now called Mount Carmel.

57

in the expedition, and all help. The men ride (horseback) and the women drive the carts. The children make the fires and do chores for the women. The men shoot buffalo; the women dry the meat and make it into pemmican . . . .

The sun set when we were still five miles from the river. Another axle had broken and heavy clouds threatened instant rain. Some advised halting; but the desire to see the Saskatchewan was too strong to be resisted, and we pushed on at a rattling rate over the rutty uneven road. Never were buckboards tested more severely and no carts but those of the Red River could have stood for ten minutes the bumps from hillock to hillock, over boulders, roots and holes, as we dashed forward at a breakneck rate [probably six or seven miles an hour!]. The last mile was downhill. The doctor and the chief put their horses to the gallop, and only drew rein when, right beneath, they saw the shining waters of the river. The rest of us were scarcely a minute behind, and three rousing cheers sent back the news to the carts. In twelve working days we had travelled five hundred and six miles, doing on this last, forty-six; and the horses looked as fresh as at the beginning of the journey; a fact that establishes the nutritious properties of the grasses, their only food on the way, as well as the strength and hardihood of the breed.

FIG. 17—*Large slough with low marshy shore in the Humboldt district. Note the native vegetation. A tall sedge, Scirpus validus, grows at the edge of the open water.*

58

Fig. 18—*A small party of half-breeds camped on the open prairie.*

The next day Fleming and his party crossed the South Saskatchewan and pushed on to Fort Carlton, where they were hospitably welcomed by Mr. Clark, the factor in charge there at that time. We will leave them here to continue their journey westward and turn to the experiences of another C.P.R. party.

E. W. JARVIS

In the late autumn of 1874 E. W. Jarvis was selected to make a winter exploration of the Smoky River Pass for the Canadian Pacific Railway Company. He had two white men and six Indians to assist him. They traveled on foot and had their supplies drawn by dog teams. As they traveled, Jarvis or his chief assistant would follow the rear sled, making a "track survey"; that is, measuring the distance by pacing, forty paces on the average being considered equal to one chain. After much strenuous traveling and the endurance of intense cold and short rations they reached Edmonton early in April. Taking charge of a packet of mail for Fort Garry they left Edmonton April the seventh and proceeded to Fort Pitt with saddle and pack horses. At Fort Pitt they secured Red River carts but the snow-banks were still deep in places and they had to break a path to let the carts through the snow for long stretches at a time. It froze so hard on certain nights, however, that the crust on the snow bore the weight of carts and horses for many miles as they approached Fort Carlton, which they reached on April the twenty-ninth. Here they were hospitably treated by the factor, Mr. Clark. At this place they were told that when the ice broke up the water had risen to a very high level with great rapidity and had carried off the scow used as a ferry. Also it had trapped a dozen Indians who had been making maple sugar on an island twenty-five miles down river, and although they had succeeded in climbing trees above the flood, they could not be rescued and all had perished by falling into the river as they became numbed with the cold.

Having secured fresh horses and bought some barley from the Prince Albert settlement, on which to help feed the horses, they started out for Fort Garry by the Carlton Trail. The following is Mr. Jarvis' account of their trip (14):

On the morning of May 5th we climbed the hill behind the Fort and set our faces towards the rising sun. The snow was nearly all gone, and we easily avoided the few remaining drifts. We reached the South Branch of the Saskatchewan the same afternoon, and spent from three to four hours making two trips across with the scow, as a strong south-west wind [down river] necessitated the hauling of the scow a long way up on our side to ensure making a good landing on the other side. At the French half-breed settle-ment here the people were driven out of their houses by the rising waters, which seem to have been higher this spring than for many years past. The grass having been all burnt off last autumn, gives the country a cheerless aspect; and we had to go to the margins of lakes or swamps to find any feed at all for the horses; but they, pushing on at the rate of thirty miles a day, with the characteristic endurance of Indian ponies, did not seem to feel the hardships of the trip as much as we had expected.

About forty-five miles from the South Branch we passed the "Spathanaw" or Round Hill, a conspicuous feature in the landscape, with a wooden crucifix on the summit said to have been placed there by a worthy Bishop who spent Sunday at its foot. Not far from here, a road branches off to the south-west, crossing the South Branch above where we did, and here we met the first appearance of civilized usages — a finger post with the following inscription:

```
┌─────────────────────────────────────────────┐
│                        ⎧ Cart.........1s. 6d. │
│   Gabriel's crossing ⎨ Waggon....2   0       │
│                        ⎩ Horses......    6     │
│        Traverse de Gabriel Dumont.            │
│                                               │
│  ▷L ⊐°ᑲᑐ°  ⋎" ▷ᑕ⋎⁻  ▽ᐃᑕ ⌐•  ⫸⫸⫸⟶            │
└─────────────────────────────────────────────┘
```

The latter statement was especially interesting; but we took it for granted that those for whom it is intended can make more out of it than we could; so we went our way and reached Touchwood Hill Post on the evening of the 9th. Here we left one of the hired horses, and as the others were already showing decided symptoms of "giving out" we had to continue the journey on foot, without even the occasional rest of a mile or two in the saddle, the animals having to be spared for use in the carts. But, wearing only moccasins, we found the unaccustomed exercise beginning to tell upon us at the end of a hundred miles, and by the time we had accomplished fifty more, were so footsore that we were quite ready to avail ourselves of a seat in a cart for half an hour when the half-starved horse seemed in a livelier mood than usual. A couple of days above Fort Ellice, we met two travellers, by name of Livingstone and Fraser, footing their way towards the mountains, thence intending to strike for the Cariboo mines. They jogged along in primitive style, unencumbered by either blanket or provisions, carrying only a spare shirt, a gun and some ammunition. To save the necessity for a blanket. and also to avoid the heat, they slept by day and marched by night. On the evening of the fourteenth we encamped at the mouth of the Qu'Appelle River, and crossed over to Fort

Ellice early next morning; ten days making the three hundred and sixteen miles from Carlton. Here we received every kind of assistance from Mr. McDonald, the gentleman in charge, who, having no available horses of his own, endeavoured to replenish our scanty stock by hiring and purchasing for us from others. We made but a short halt, crossing the Assiniboine on the scow after dinner — the bridge having been carried away by the freshet — and pushed on a dozen miles to the east over a very good road. In saying goodbye to Mr. McDonald, we parted with regret with the last of a number of gentlemen, officers of the Hon. Hudson's Bay Company, who have shown us every kindness and extended a ready hospitality on every occasion we have come in contact with them. To most if not all of them, we were personally unknown; but it was sufficient to say we were in need of help, to ensure at once their best endeavours on our behalf.

We were delayed until ten o'clock next morning, as our horses had seen fit to rejoin their companions near the Fort, but we got past Shoal Lake before camping time. In crossing the Little Saskatchewan River we had a good deal of trouble, the water was very swift and high, being above the horses' backs. The load had to be piled on an improvised rack on top of the cart body, and by an ingenious

Fig. 19—*Dysart, Sask., a thriving town now standing in one of the districts explored by Macoun in 1879.*

combination of tow lines, the horse swimming and the cart afloat, they were safely piloted across. This was our last excitement, except the breaking of an axle against a stump a few miles further on, and we soon reached the flourishing settlement at the third, second, and first crossings of the White Mud River, where the farmers were busy with their spring occupations, but not over-sanguine of success, owing to the annual scourge of grasshoppers, which has hitherto turned this fruitful colony into a barren waste.

Passing Portage la Prairie on the 19th, we reached Winnipeg on the 21st of May, having been five and a half months on our trip. At White Horse Plains we met a gay cavalcade going westward; it consisted of Mr. McLeod and his two survey parties, just starting for Edmonton and the Rocky Mountains, and their shining boots, glittering spurs and well-groomed horses contrasted with our battered and weather-worn appearance. But we could afford to suffer by the comparison; they would soon be as ragged as we were, and all their troubles were before them, while we were just reaching the goal, pushed forward to over many a weary mile of mountain and plain, and could take our well-earned repose in the happy consciousness of having fulfilled the task allotted to us, and earned the approbation of him we are proud to acknowledge our chief.

JOHN MACOUN

One of the most interesting characters who ever traveled the Carlton Trail was John Macoun, an early prophet of Western Canada's greatness as an agricultural land. Quite by chance he was picked up by Sandford Fleming and brought along as botanist to his party in 1872. After following the Carlton Trail from Fort Garry to Carlton they continued on to Edmonton, where the party divided. Horetsky and Macoun were detailed to go to the Peace River country and pass through the mountains to Fort McLeod and then proceed from that place on to the coast. They left Edmonton early in September and followed the route prescribed but parted company at Fort St. James. Macoun proceeded on to the Fraser River and down to the Coast and over to Victoria where he spent Christmas. Continuing on to San Francisco by boat and to Chicago via the Union Pacific

FIG. 20—*One of the posts that were used by the North West Mounted Police shortly after they were established in Northwest Territories.*

Railway he finally reached Ontario early in the new year. After writing a report of his journey for the authorities at Ottawa he returned to his position as teacher of natural history in Albert College, Belleville, Ontario.

In the spring of 1875 Macoun again went West, this time under the direction of Dr. Selwyn. He traveled by way of California to Victoria, where his duties began. Regarding these he says (19):

> I had been appointed botanist to the party with instructions to make note on all the country passed through, in regard to the flora, the climate, and agricultural capabilities. This I performed to the best of my ability from Victoria to Peace River Pass, and the whole length of the Peace River, and nearly one thousand miles before I reached Fort Carlton on the prairie.

Pressing on over the Carlton Trail he reached Winnipeg on November the third and arrived back in the East on November the thirteenth, 1875.

Four years later Macoun again went West to lead a small

exploring party over some of the more open country in the Northwest Territories (Fig. 19). He reached Winnipeg about the middle of May and took a river steamboat up to Fort Ellice with his men and supplies. After leaving the Hudson's Bay post his party followed the Carlton Trail for a few days and then struck across the trackless prairie to the Elbow of the South Saskatchewan River via the north end of Last Mountain Lake. At the Elbow they crossed the river and traveled to the Hand Hills and on to Calgary before returning home via Battleford and Winnipeg.

The following year, 1880, he led a party to the Moose Mountains, then across the Souris Plains to the present site of Moose Jaw, then on to Old Wives Lake and the Cypress Hills. There he visited the Mounted Police post, known as Fort Walsh (Fig. 20), and was advised to keep his horses with those of the Mounted Police during his visit to prevent the Indians from stealing them. Turning northeast at this point he traveled past the Elbow of the South Saskatchewan nearly to Humboldt before returning to Winnipeg by way of the Anglican mission on the Gordon Indian Reserve and Fort Ellice.

In 1881 Macoun made his last expedition for the purpose of spying out the land. That summer he and his little party struggled through the lake and bush country of what is now western Manitoba and eastern Saskatchewan. They traveled largely by boat and ascended the Red Deer River for some distance and then crossed over to the headwaters of the Swan River and descended it to Livingstone, which was then a post of the North West Mounted Police with Inspector Griesbach in charge. From here they traveled across country to Fort Pelly and then continued by boat down the Assiniboine to Fort Ellice. Then they proceeded to Brandon on foot with the aid of a half-breed to guide them and a cart to carry their luggage. One day's travel brought them to the advance construction gang at work on the new transcontinental railway, and three days' travel

65

brought them to the new town of Brandon, where they were able to take a train for the East. After each trip he wrote a full report of the country examined (18, 19, 20). All his reports spoke in enthusiastic terms of the boundless possibilities for agricultural development (Fig. 21) in the vast new land.

John Macoun was now given a permanent position with the government. His future work consisted mainly of collecting and arranging, in a museum of natural history, plant and bird collections from all over Canada. Thus in later years he was able, on some of his collecting trips, to revisit the Prairies and see the fulfillment of his early prophesies and dreams in the marvelous agricultural progress which took place in Western Canada between 1880 and 1910. Before turning to other men connected with the history of the Carlton Trail let us examine a few excerpts from Macoun's own writings. The first three have to do with his journey over the Carlton Trail in the summer of 1872 in company with Sandford Fleming:

I may as well mention now our mode of travel. Our caravan con-

FIG. 21—*Fields of ripe golden wheat in the "park country."*

sisted of six Red River carts and two buckboards which had been bought at St. Paul. The carts were all of wood and no iron in them at all. From this time forward, the chief decided that we would make three spells a day and must make at least forty miles each day for the next month. We had attached to one of the carts an odometer, which gave the number of revolutions of the wheel, and from that was measured the distance travelled on each spell. By such means, we knew without any difficulty how many miles we had travelled. The cavalcade was arranged so that one buckboard went in front and then the six carts one after the other. My buckboard was the last of all. We had over forty horses and, as we were going so fast most of the time, they were changed three times a day. This was our regular mode of travelling for the whole trip. We would rise at sunrise and have some breakfast; take a second breakfast after going about ten to fifteen miles; then take our mid-day spell of the same distance and, after dinner, take another spell and camp early in the evening. As we were passing over the whole distance through the "fertile belt," we were seldom on a very extensive prairie so that we had feed, wood, and water most of the time.

The next passages show why Grant in *Ocean to Ocean,* (9) always referred to John Macoun as "the Botanist." They describe a district in Manitoba where the trail rises from the first to the second prairie steppe:

For eight miles the trail led through a rich country, vegetation of every kind most luxuriant. The whole of this region was evidently covered with forest at no distant date, as there were still oaks and many aspens remaining. Fires were gradually denuding the whole country of wood, as the margins of all groves show the action of fires. Passing out of this we came to a region of sand dunes. Here we observed the first coniferous trees seen since leaving Oak Point. White spruce (Abies alba), common juniper (Juniperus communis) and the creeping variety (J. Sabina var. procumbens) were abundant, and underneath their shade grew many of the flowers of the pine woods of Canada. Pine Creek, a small stream, winds amongst those hills which stretch for about four miles on either side of the stream. Gradually the hills melt into the plain, and a wide dry prairie extending for miles spreads out before us. The soil is well suited for cultivation, but wood is very scarce. About the centre of this prairie we crossed Boggy Creek [White Mud River], and six miles beyond came to a gravelly tract thickly strewn with boulders. For twenty-one miles the surface of the country is much diversified by ponds, lakelets, small groves of aspen, and thickets of willows, with broad, dry expanses of prairie, covered with grass and flowers. Since we struck the hill, we have been gradually rising higher and higher, and the vegetation shows a drier climate. We are now on the banks of the Little Saskatchewan [Minnedosa River], which runs in a valley about 200 feet deep: evidently scooped out of the drift by its own water. The leading characteristics of the vegetation remain unbroken. On low spots sedge grass (Carex) mixed with wheat grass (Triticum), cord grass (Spartina), and various species of blue joint (Calamagrostis). On the dry grounds the grasses are various species of Vilfa, Sporobolus, and Stipa, with a few others in less abundance. The chief flowering plants are wild bergamot (Monarda fistulosa), various sunflowers (Helianthus), Cone flowers (Rudbeckia), Golden Rods (Solidago), and a multitude of Asters, Petalostemons, Lupinus, Oxytropus, Hedysarum, and many fine species of Astragalus with other Leguminous and Rosaceous plants. The valley of the river is very beautiful and formed a pleasing contrast to the monotonous country passed over before reaching it. The timber on its banks is nearly all destroyed by the recklessness of travellers. In a few years there will not be a tree left in the country. From the river, the country still kept ascending, ridge after ridge coming into view until at last we reached the level of the steppe. Before reaching this the vegetation showed a considerable retardation, owing to the want of heat and moisture; except this, there was no change. We camped for the night at the Salt Lakes, which are in a slight depression, off the general level of the plateau. The shores of the lakes produce many saline plants, of which the following are the principal: Scirpus maritimus, Salicornia herbacea, Glaux maritima, Suada maritima, Glyceria distans; these have a wide range over the whole interior wherever salt lakes are found.

The whole distance between Rat Creek and Fort Carlton, a tract of over 350 miles, is remarkable for the sameness of its flora. Very little change was noted after crossing the Assiniboine, except a few plants peculiar to sandy soils. The hill-top, the plain, the marsh, the aspen copse, the willow thicket—each had its own flora throughout the whole region, never varying and scarcely ever becoming inter-mixed. Even the fresh water ponds could be noted by their grasses being different from those bordering the saline ones. That there is a great uniformity respecting soil, humidity, and temperature throughout this whole region is apparent from the unvarying character of its natural productions. How much of it is suited for the purposes of agriculture, a hurried ride through it cannot show. But this much was seen, that wherever the soil or the natural contour of the land would interfere with the raising of grain, immense herds of cattle, droves of horses and flocks of sheep could be raised. This taken in connection with the immense herds of buffalo that formerly grazed on those boundless plains, should cause the most skeptical to form a higher estimate of the value of this far off land. It requires very little prophetical skill to enable anyone to foretell that very few years will elapse before this region will be teeming with flocks and herds. [Fig. 22]

The following paragraph refers to his stop at Fort Carlton on his way home from the Peace River country in 1875:

I rested two days at Fort Carlton and, in the meantime, had the pleasure of meeting Capt. Crozier, of the Northwest Mounted

FIG. 22—*Some of the farm animals envisioned by John Macoun in this fertile portion of Western Canada.*

Police, who had been a Lieutenant in the company in which I served at Prescott, in 1866. We were pleased to see each other and Mr. Clark, the gentleman in charge of Carlton, invited us both to dine with him that evening. Besides the Captain and myself, there were two priests, one of whom was named Père Andreau [André]. While taking dinner, we were discussing the future of the country and Père Andreau [André] said that he was going to bring a large number of half-breeds from Manitoba to settle on the Saskatchewan and form a new French province. After dinner I told Captain Crozier that I would make a note of what the priest had said as it meant trouble in the future and that I would advise him to do the same. Whether he did so or not I cannot say, but he commanded the Northwest Mounted Police at the battle of Duck Lake, the first engagement in the rebellion of 1885.

A couple of incidents which occurred on the trip from Carlton to Fort Garry are included here:

One morning, when we were about to start, I decided to remain behind and write up my notes and was busily engaged when I became poetical and had just written: "I think I hear the tramp of the coming millions," and, as I had reached this period, a concert broke out a few yards behind me, and, on looking around, I saw a line of coyotes sitting on a ridge and giving their peculiar howl. I need scarcely add that I never became poetical again. When I mentioned it to the men, they said that coyotes always followed a party of half-breeds when on the trail to pick up the refuse of the camp when they had left.

It was the month of October and as they traveled along the Carlton Trail they met cold weather and snow. Regarding one of the camps along the way he wrote:

Our fine weather continued until the evening of the 23rd of October when it began to thicken up and the next morning we were off long before daylight, but, as the day broke we saw that we were in for a snowstorm. We halted in a little clump of willows and had a cup of tea. We had scarcely started again when the storm broke and, in a few minutes, the air was filled with driving snow. For the next sixteen miles there was neither bush nor tree, and for the whole of this distance we tramped against a furious gale and driving storm. Late in the afternoon of the 24th, we reached the timber and, under the direction of our experienced guide, penetrated to a little marsh

70

surrounded by wood, and camped. We could hear the roar of the gale outside, but not a breath stirred where we were. There was fine pasture for the horses and cattle in the marsh and we had no difficulty in making ourselves comfortable. In a short time we had blazing fires and, after the ice was thawed off our clothes, we sat about the fire making a shelter for the night. I lay under the wagon with my feet to the fire and was so comfortable that I never wakened until the morning.

The following excerpt is taken from Macoun's account of his start from Fort Ellice in 1879, when he came up the Assiniboine River by steamboat:

Without accident we reached Fort Ellice and all our possessions were placed on the bank and we took possession and carried them up to the prairie above. My man was there with the horses (all the way from Winnipeg), and we erected our tents and got our things under cover as soon as possible. We had three tents—one for myself and nephew, another for Mr. Wilkins and his brother-in-law and another for Matheson and Ogilvie. When we had all our belongings together and our four carts and two buckboards, my assistant, Wilkins, came to me and said: "Professor, we will never be able to take all this stuff on our conveyances; we simply cannot do it under any circumstances." I knew now was my time to assert myself and I said: "Boys, from what Mr. Wilkins says there is some doubt as to our ability to take all our stuff with us and I wish to tell you that 'can't' is not in my vocabulary and the man who uses it on this trip can consider himself dismissed. The boat has not gone back yet and any man who wishes to return is at liberty to do so at once, but I wish to tell you that, from this time forth, any man who thinks he knows more about his work than I do ceases to be an employee of mine."

As a sequel to this little episode he has the following to say about their activities the next morning:

My next order was to separate all the men's belongings. Mr. Wilkins and myself were to take everything that belonged to us on our buckboards and, to each of the men, I assigned a cart and he packed his share of the stuff in it in his own way with the under-standing that whatever was in the cart could be got at the shortest notice. In other words, our men must know where each article that he had in his cart was placed. My reason for doing this was that I

71

had a spade, an axe, a shearing-hook, and many other small articles that might be wanted for instant use, and I desired each man to be aware of what he carried. When we began to tie up our stuff and fix it all, we found that we had room enough for all we had.

One fine portion of the new land was bounded on the east by the 102nd meridian, on the south by the Qu'Appelle Valley, on the west by Last Mountain Lake, on the northwest by a line from the north end of Last Mountain Lake to the Quill Lakes, and on the north by a line from these lakes to Fort Pelly. This area was bisected diagonally by the Carlton Trail. Regarding this large district Macoun had the following things to say (21):

This tract of country contains at least 7,000 square miles, or about four and a half million acres of excellent soil. It is true that the western side is almost devoid of wood, but to compensate, the hills, extending along its flank, are covered with trees. Proceeding northward of the travelled road [i.e. the Carlton Trail], the country becomes more broken, ponds and marshes are numerous and wood increases in both size and quality, until it merges into continuous forest south of the present telegraph line. A rich black loam about fifteen inches in depth, containing small grains of quartz or other rock, is the prevailing surface soil, but this imperceptibly passes into lighter colored sandy loam, as the timber becomes more continuous and of larger growth. The subsoil is generally a lighter colored marly clay, but this again, in the ridges, passes into gravel, which is generally gneiss covered with a coating of carbonate of lime. . . . Abundance of good water is found on every part of this tract for the greater part of the summer, and future settlers will find that good permanent wells can be obtained, at a reasonable depth, on any part of the prairie. Poplar wood for house-building, fencing, and firewood, can easily be procured at Pheasant, File and Touchwood Hills, which extend from southeast to northwest through its whole extent. Almost continuous woods extend along the Carlton Road from twelve miles east of its western boundary to where the Qu'Appelle and Pelly Road crosses it. Thence eastward extends the Pheasant Plain, a stretch of twenty-five miles long, without wood, but Pheasant Hills having abundance of it, are always in sight. East and northeast of this plain, copse wood is more or less abundant, until the Assiniboine is reached. . . . While encamped at the head of Last Mountain Lake in 1879, we had ample opportunity to ex-

FIG. 23—*The Quill Plains along Highway No. 6, just south of Dafoe. Note the high water table.*

amine this part of the country. We were particularly charmed with its soil, productions, and position. Multitudes of pelican, geese, ducks, avocets, phalaropes, water hens, and grebe, besides innumerable snipe and plover were everywhere in the marshes at the head of the lake or along its shores, or on small islands lying to the south of the camp. This was early in July and experience tells me that not one-tenth was then seen of the bird life assembled in September and October.

Extending west from the Touchwood Hills, is a level plain [Fig. 23] without wood for thirty miles on the line of the Carlton Trail. This plain has been erroneously called the Great Salt Plain, whereas the part of it to which the term applies, is scarcely twelve miles wide on the trail . . . . There is undoubtedly a saline depression extending from Quill Lakes to Long Lake, the worst parts of which are largely made up of white mud swamps or brackish marshes, but there are no data to show that it covers twenty per cent of the area assigned to it.

THE TELEGRAPH LINE

An innovation having some connection with the Carlton Trail was the long telegraph line from Winnipeg to Edmonton (22). For a time, it followed the original survey of the first

73

transcontinental railway, passing from Selkirk across the narrows of Lake Manitoba, through Livingstone, Humboldt, Clark's Crossing, and Battleford. The eastern section from Selkirk to Livingstone, a place twelve miles from Pelly, was built and in operation by July, 1876. The western section was completed to Leduc by November of the same year. It was finally extended to Edmonton early in 1879. After crossing the Carlton Trail at Humboldt the telegraph line followed closely the route of the present railway from Humboldt to Langham but continued on up to Battleford on the south side of the North Saskatchewan River. There were several so-called "stations" along the line, at each of which was an operator and a lineman. For the first few years, George Weldon served as lineman, and his wife as operator, at Humboldt. Many travelers became acquainted with these hospitable people and held them in high esteem. Their station was about five miles west and two miles south of the present townsite.

Much trouble was experienced in keeping the line in operation. The eastern part passed through a lot of low marshy land and woods, and in the west, the buffalo pushed over many of the poles rubbing their shaggy sides against them. At times prairie fires burned down a great many of the posts which supported the wire. Owing to the change in the routing of the C.P.R. the portion of the original telegraph line, east of Humboldt, was abandoned about 1881 and new lines, from South Qu'Appelle to Humboldt and from Clark's Crossing to Prince Albert, up the west side to the river, were completed by the fall of 1883. At times business over the line was very slack, especially during periods when the wire was down in places. On occasion checker matches were played between checker enthusiasts of Battleford, Edmonton, and Qu'Appelle; also medical advice was dispensed up and down the line from a medical book in the telegraph office at Battleford. However, in the spring of 1885 the telegraph line really proved its worth and the wires were kept hot throughout the period of the rebellion. It was an important factor in the suppression of the disturbance.

A telegraph station was established in the Touchwood Hills at Kutawa in 1883. Mr. Von Lindeburgh was placed in charge of this station and the central section of the line between South Qu'Appelle and Humboldt, and he continued to look after it until the line was finally dismantled in 1922. While he was away inspecting and repairing the line, his wife acted as operator. One of the most difficult parts of his beat was the stretch across the Quill Plains. In the winter he would load his repair kit on a horse-drawn sled, together with supplies of bacon, bannock and tea, and travel his beat, sleeping in the open. At times he carried bandages for his horse's legs to protect them from the crust on the surface of the deep snow. About 1908, when the main line of the Grand Trunk Pacific Railway was being built through the Touchwood Hills, Mr. Lindeburgh did a rushing business sending and receiving messages for the men of the construction camps. The railway passed within about five miles of Kutawa. The importance of the government line decreased rapidly after this railway with its accompanying telegraph line was completed, but the old line continued to function to some extent for another fourteen years or so.

JAMES TROW

James Trow was chairman of the immigration and colonization committee of the Canadian House of Commons in 1877. In the summer and autumn of that year he made a tour of parts of Manitoba and the Northwest Territories. He was inspecting the country with a view to deciding in his own mind its suitability for agricultural settlement. All through his account (43) of his trip this topic is uppermost in his mind. However, he produced a very readable story of what he saw and heard and in the light of later developments, his opinions and prophecies are most interesting.

Mr. Trow started out from Winnipeg, accompanied by his son, on August the fourth and a few days later an old acquaintance, named Moss, who had settled in Manitoba, joined them for the trip. Between them they had a team of mules, a fine team of Indian ponies, a Red River cart and a buckboard. Apparently Mr. Moss was a resourceful individual who could cook, hunt, repair broken vehicles, and make himself generally useful; in short, he was an excellent man to have along on such a journey.

First of all it may be well to outline the route which they followed. They went by the old Trail to Fort Ellice and on towards the Touchwood Hills until they came to a trail which branched off to Lebret and Fort Qu'Appelle. They followed this and after visiting Fort Qu'Appelle they went north on a trail to the mission now on the Gordon Reserve in the Little Touchwood Hills. From the mission they took a trail which brought them back to the Carlton Trail near the point where the first Hudson's Bay post in the Touchwood Hills used to stand. Following the Carlton Trail to Humboldt they took the left branch which followed the telegraph line in a westerly direction for a time, and then passed north of Muskiki Lake near Bremen and crossed the South Saskatchewan at Gabriel's Crossing. After visiting Fort Carlton they went to the Prince Albert settlement. On their return journey they traveled southwest past Red Deer Hill and the half-breed colony of St. Laurent, joining the old Trail at Batoche from whence they took the other branch back to Humboldt. After reaching the site of the first Hudson's Bay post in the Touchwood Hills they continued along the Carlton Trail passing the third post, which remained in operation until 1909. In fact they followed the original line of the Carlton Trail all the way from Batoche to Winnipeg except where diversions occurred in the settled parts of Manitoba. They arrived back at Winnipeg about the middle of October after having traveled over 1,600 miles.

During the trip Mr. Trow met a number of noted men and saw many interesting sights. At Silver Heights, just west of Winnipeg, he saw thoroughbred horses and domesticated buffalo belonging to the Hon. Jas. Mackay. At the home of the Hon. D. A. Smith he noted preparations for the entertainment of the Governor General of Canada. At Portage la Prairie he visited the home of Mr. Kenneth McKenzie, who was a farmer and also a member of the provincial legislature. After traveling through comparatively well-settled districts, all the way from Winnipeg to a point some distance west of Portage la Prairie, he mentions passing isolated settlers and small colonies further westward. For instance, at the first of the Three Creeks, he mentions a Mr. McKinnon whose nearest neighbor to the east was twenty-four miles away, while to the west it was eighty miles to Tanner's, on the Little Saskatchewan River. The year 1877 was one of high precipitation in Manitoba and Mr. Trow makes many references to the high level of the water and the difficulty experienced in crossing the lowlands and creeks in the province. He also mentions two toll bridges, one over the Little Saskatchewan and one over the Assiniboine River. At the former stream they were met and questioned by Captain French of the Mounted Police regarding any liquor which they might have in their possession. Near Shoal Lake, at the spot where a trail branched off for Fort Pelly, they found Col. Richardson and his family encamped. The Colonel and his family were on their way to Battleford where he was to serve as stipendiary magistrate. When Mr. Trow and his companions reached Fort Ellice they found that hundreds of Indians had gathered there to receive the annual payments of money and goods accruing to them by the terms of Treaty No. 4, which was negotiated in 1874. They found Mr. Archie McDonald in charge of the Hudson's Bay post. His thoughts were now turning from the fur trade to the supplying of settlers' requirements, the disposal of Hudson's Bay Company lands, and the need of railways to aid in developing the resources of the Northwest. During his stay at Fort Ellice, Mr. Trow heard Archdeacon Cowley preach to the Indians, with Mr. Pratt, a well-educated Cree Indian, acting as interpreter. Mr. Pratt was living in the valley at Qu'Appelle when Dr. Hector, of Palliser's Expedition, visited that place in 1857. Here is Mr. Trow's description of the service:

The chiefs and a large number of their bands attended, and squatted on the ground inside the tent. The Indians conducted themselves in an orderly manner, and would frequently applaud the speaker with a grunt——hoh, hoh. The squaws were not admitted into the tent; poor creatures, they were all busily engaged in dressing hides, repairing tents, making fancy bead work or gathering fuel. The Indians were inveterate smokers, and the odour emitted from that horrid weed they smoke [the dried bark of the red willow, called kinnikanic] is very unpleasant. They smoked during the delivery of the sermon. A headsman would fill a large stone pipe having a stem two and a half to three feet long, and this pipe was handed to the chief, who took a few graceful puffs and handed it to the next in rank, and so on round the circle. After the pipe returned to the chief it was again replenished by the headsman and sent on its mission of peace. The tent in which the service was held was covered with buffalo robes, 24 in number on the lower tier. The poles coming together at the top left scarcely any room for ventilation. The Indians sat round with a blanket or robe covering their loins, their bodies to the waist perfectly bare; many of the leaders were tattooed all over the breast.

Concerning the payment of the treaty money he says:

On Monday morning I accompanied Capt. McDonald, paymaster, to the Indian encampments. The natives gathered round his tent like bees around a hive, anxiously waiting for their little pittance in money and provisions. The contractor having killed and distributed among them a dozen oxen that morning, the paymaster opened his cash box. The natives presented their little brass tokens, and received their respective amounts. The greatest harmony prevailed, although occasionally a little bickering would take place when claiming pay for so many wives and children. Polygamy seems to prevail to an alarming extent. Many have two, three, or more wives, and for each they are entitled to $5.00. The sum total paid foots up to precisely the same amount in the aggregate, whether the Indian has one wife or ten, but the moral effect is bad. In the evening, numbers of the natives assembled in one of the chief's wigwams for the purpose of seeing Capt. McDonald present to the chiefs and headsmen, new suits of clothing. One of the chiefs, named White Bear, a very corpulent, elderly man, requested Capt. McDonald to allow him to present his son, young White Bear, with the suit designed for him; that he was getting feeble and it was his desire and the wish of the whole tribe that his son should put on his mantle. Capt. McDonald made an excellent and appropriate speech. The chiefs put off their robes, stood erect, and each made suitable reply. After this ceremony we all assisted in dressing the chiefs and headsmen in their gaudy new attire, but failed to convince them of the utility of a pair of pants. The party afterwards escorted the captain in military style to his headquarters at the Fort.

At Fort Qu'Appelle they found a huge assemblage of over 5,000 Indians with 500 teepees awaiting the arrival of the paymaster. Affairs did not run so smoothly here, for the Indians were dissatisfied with the quality and quantity of provisions issued to them. However, after some days of stalling and arguing they accepted their payments and provisions. These included 25,000 pounds of pemmican and three or four hundred sacks of flour. At that time there were five men at the mounted police post in Fort Qu'Appelle under the command of Capt. Griesbach. Mr. McLean was in charge of the Hudson's Bay post.

After leaving Fort Qu'Appelle, Mr. Trow wrote:

We travelled during the day 35 miles, and in the evening we camped near Child's Mountain, a spur of the Little Touchwood Hills. The water of the little lake adjoining was somewhat dark but drinkable. We took an early start next morning and in a few hours arrived at an Indian or half-breed settlement. All the males were out hunting buffalo on the plains for their winter supplies. One of the half-breeds had the previous day killed a stray buffalo bull. Aged buffalo bulls are often found at great distances from the herd—occasionally three or four together, and are easily slaughtered. A short distance beyond we arrived at the English church mission, under the charge of Rev. Joseph Reader. The mission buildings stand on the brow

FIG. 24—*Anglican mission on the Gordon Indian Reserve, about seven miles south of Punnichy. The lake was nearly dry when this photograph was taken in July, 1949.*

of a hill, fronting a beautiful little lake [Fig. 24]. The missionary has under cultivation a few acres, and the vegetables and roots in the garden were excellent. Several half-breeds reside in the neighbourhood and cultivate small patches. The Government furnished them with grain and potatoes. The soil is a rich loam. The vegetables were much earlier than I expected and of extraordinary growth. I mounted a ladder or frame scaffolding attached to the stockade of the mission, and from the observatory I obtained a magnificient view of the surrounding country. To the south and south-west I looked across an extensive prairie, with occasional elevations or hills dotted promiscuously here and there, as if to embellish the scenery, and away beyond the view extends to the valley of the Qu'Appelle. The Last Mountain is also seen to the south-west but distant many leagues from the position it is represented on the map. To the east among the trees can be seen the mission schoolhouse kept by Mr. Settee. Away in the west, Heart's Hill is seen towering above all the rest, and, far beyond it, the great salt plains. The whole country presents a lovely appearance;

abundance of good timber, sufficiently large for building purposes is seen to the north of the mission. . . . Rev. Mr. Reader seems perfectly contented with his isolated position, shut out from society and civilization. He complains, however, that there are no regular postal privileges. It is only by chance that he can correspond with his friends and acquaintances. The previous day he had received a letter from a relative residing in England, bearing date July 1876, it having been over 13 months in reaching its destination.

Describing his experience in crossing the South Saskatchewan, Mr. Trow wrote:

After preparing breakfast, we started for the river — two hour's drive. We arrived at the Ferry [Gabriel's Crossing], and having no horn, whistled for Gabriel, for we could not see twenty feet in front [because of a dense fog]. The ferryman soon appeared, and made preparation for crossing. The boat was a flat-bottomed scow, roughly put together. Our animals were unhitched, the carriage and cart put in the centre of the boat, the mules on one side, the horses on the other. Gabriel gave instructions by signs and some doubtful French. The mules were very obstinate and troublesome to put on board. He had probably been more accustomed to oxen than mules and undertook to twist the tail of one of the mules. Instantly he received a kick below the ribs, in that portion of the body called by pugilists "the bread basket." Each of our party undertook to row with an unyielding oar, first keeping along the shore and working upstream; fortunately the wind was favorable, which counteracted the force of the rapid current. The river has a swift current, and is probably over 200 yards in width at low water, with an average depth of 8 to 15 feet. The fee paid Gabriel was $1.50 for ourselves, horses and carriages.

While at Fort Carlton, then in charge of Mr. Clark, he wrote:

I met at the Fort Mr. Wm. McKay, agent at Fort Pitt, and others who had just arrived from Battleford. They stated that Mr. Sutherland and his workmen had just completed the Parliament buildings, Governor's residence, offices, and residences for the several Government officials—some 22 buildings in all. They were reported to be finished in splendid style.

About the middle of September they visited the settlement of Prince Albert. Here they found that some 750 pioneers were scattered along the south side of the North Saskatchewan River for a distance of about twenty-five miles. The settlement possessed Wesleyan, Presbyterian and Church of England missions, two good schools, and a grist mill, saw mill, and shingle mill run by steam power. Cereals, potatoes, and other vegetables were producing remarkably well. The settlers had about 8,500 horses and cattle and considerable farm machinery brought in at great expense. They were finding poultry raising rather difficult because of the ravages of wolves and Indian dogs. Here he met Capt. Moore, an Irish gentleman of considerable means, who had joined the colony and had brought in the machinery for the various mills all the way from Ontario.

After leaving Prince Albert they went down to Batoche through the Métis settlement of St. Laurent. Of this place he wrote:

The soil here is much lighter than at Prince Albert. We drove from house to house for information respecting the crossing, but to our astonishment the settlement was deserted, and the doors and windows were locked or nailed up. After many unsuccessful attempts along the numerous trails, at last we arrived at the mission and found Father Foremond at home—"monarch of all he surveyed." This gentleman was alone, the only male inhabitant that could be found for miles. Fathers, mothers, sons, and daughters, absolutely all excepting a few old men and young children, were away to the plains with their horses, cattle and dogs; hunting the buffalo and preparing their winter supplies. The younger members of the family take charge of the stock, the father and oldest sons chase and kill the buffalo, the mothers and daughters prepare the pemmican and dried meat, and tan and cure the robes. Many of these hunters are satisfied with supplies sufficient for the year; others remain longer and return with loads for sale to white settlers and traders. The French half-breeds are very indifferent farmers; they love a roaming, exciting life, are fond of the dance and assembling for fun and frolic. . . . I produced my credentials—a letter of introduction from his Grace Archbishop Taché—to Father Foremond, who very kindly invited myself and party to dinner. Letting out our animals

FIG. 25—*Catholic church at St. Laurent, July, 1951.*

we took a stroll through the church property, while the reverend father prepared the dinner, for he was a man of all work. Father Foremond [Fourmond] is a devoted Christian minister; his very appearance would convince the most skeptical that he was sincere and devoted to his charge. . . . The chapel is erected on the summit of the river bank [Fig. 25], overlooking the residences of his parishioners for miles on both sides. In front of the church on a raised platform or triangle is hung a large bell, which can be distinctly heard for miles. Near the church we found an enclosed burying ground. Down in the dingle north of the house in a sheltered nook we saw a beautiful spring boiling up.

We cannot dwell on other incidents of their return journey, but Batoche himself, then over eighty years of age, ferried them across the river and told them tales of buffalo hunting in his younger days. Just before they crossed the telegraph line they noticed the Hill of the Cross and gained a fine view from its summit. Regarding it he writes:

On the summit of the highest cone of this range of hills was erected a cross. We climbed up the steep acclivity, and from the elevated position we had an extensive view of the surrounding country. Along the north side of the mountain, at its base, there is a succession of lakes gradually growing less by the washings of sediment from the hilltops, and the growth and decay of vegetable matter.

Once their camp fire nearly started a prairie fire when a breeze sprang up at night. Before reaching the Quill Plains they met Lt. Gov. Laird and his family on their way to Battleford. Trow's party experienced both snow and delightful "Indian summer" weather before reaching Winnipeg again. In conclusion he said:

> I have satisfied myself and returned with my mind stored with many interesting and pleasant recollections of my travels, and have unbounded faith in the great future of the great North-west.

LIZZIE McFADDEN

Intimate glimpses of the trials and reactions of the rank and file of the early settlers who came into the Saskatchewan country via the Carlton Trail are afforded by the diary of Lizzie McFadden (10). Lizzie was fourteen years of age when she made the trip in the summer of 1879, and her people were on their way to settle at Prince Albert. The trip lasted from July the third to August the twenty-sixth. Had it not been for the fact that Lizzie kept a diary we would never have heard a word about the journey, but fortunately we can draw on it for a few pictures of travel by Red River cart in her day:

> Thursday, July 3rd, 1879: Left Winnipeg. The horses balked; went about a hundred yards and the harness broke and it rained about ten minutes. Two hours getting through a mudhole. Got about two miles and the cart axle broke and we had to camp for the night. [Not a very auspicious start, was it?]
>
> Monday, July 7th: It rained all Sunday night, so we did not start very early, but when we did we had splendid roads all the way and no trouble with the oxen. There were two cart trains passed us on the road. One train contained about 76 horses and carts;

crossed one creek. It was pretty deep. We camped about 7 o'clock beside some half-breeds and slept soundly all night.

Thursday, July 10th: Started to look for our oxen this morning; they got away in the night. The boys tramped all the morning and found them about five miles away. We started about ten o'clock. Had a good many mudholes to go through. Our pony got down in a hole coming through a great slough and the oxen had to pull us out. We camped on a beautiful hill with white poplar at the back of us. It is the nicest place we have seen yet. The mosquitoes are not so bad, and it is very pleasant.

Saturday, July 12th: Started at 5 o'clock in the morning and made seven miles by nine o'clock. Camped and fed the horses at High Bluff. Saw the Orangemen pass on their way to Portage la Prairie. Started again at twelve o'clock; had good roads, then we had to double over a mudhole; then had good roads all the way to Portage. Arrived there at 7 p.m. Mr. Carruthers met us as soon as we got there and I went to buy some bread. It was four loaves for 25 cents. Camped by a house and got lots of water there. Looks like rain.

Sunday, July 20th: Rested today. Very pleasant day. Baked cakes and pies all morning. Read all afternoon. A minister came to see us in the middle of our cooking. Went for a walk in the evening. Mosquitoes nearly ate us up. There were lots of trains passed us today. Cool this evening.

Saturday, July 26th: Started pretty early. Had a fearful time with the horses. Had a great many sloughs to cross. Camped and had dinner. Rested about two hours; then started and got to Shoal Lake about five miles. Had to cross the lake. It was up to the wagon box. Camped near the barracks. Had the police visiting us this evening trying to find out if we had any liquor about us.

Wednesday, July 30th; Started very early and came over 28 sloughs before dinner. After dinner we had splendid roads. When we came in view of Fort Ellice there were great hills to go up and we had to cross a bridge over the Assiniboine; then climb high hills and reach the top of them at 7 o'clock. I was frightened by some Indians on the road [Fig. 26]. Fort Ellice is a very pretty place but no farming country. It is very cool tonight.

Saturday, August 2nd: Started very early. Had a great many sand banks and sloughs to cross. Passed the McDougal [sic] party today. Mr. McDougal is going to preach tomorrow, and we are going to camp near them. Made a very big day. Mosquitoes very bad tonight. It was about nine o'clock when we camped. We are about two miles from Cut Arm Creek.

Thursday, August 7th: We are still in the Touchwood Hills and likely to be. They are very long. We have not so many sloughs as we used to have, but the roads are very rough. We have a party of half-breeds with us who are going to Prince Albert and have lots of company. They have a cow and we have lots of milk. Travelled very late tonight.

Thursday, August 14th: Started very early and crossed the [Quill] Plains. Ox is much worse today. It seems to be lamer. This morning there were two policemen passed by and in the afternoon we

FIG. 26—*Assiniboine Indian with buffalo-hide lodges. Travois are leaned against the one on the left.*

met them. One, S. J. Donaldson [subsequently the local member for Prince Albert], was sick. Mother gave him some painkiller. In the evening Hon. Matthew Ryan passed on his way to Battleford to council. We travelled very late this evening and the mosquitoes were terrifying. Pa had to come slower with the ox. Camped by Mr. Ryan's this evening.

Saturday, August 16th: The ox seems to be much worse today, so we had to travel very slowly. Passed a man going to Winnipeg from Glencoe, Ontario. He knew Uncle James well. Then we passed another man, a brother-in-law of the breed. We got to Humboldt at noon and camped there. The breeds came along and went on without us as they were in a hurry to reach Prince Albert. In the afternoon Captain Moore came to visit us. He came down from Prince Albert to telegraph. Had a visit from Maggie Leggett and brother-in-law. She brought us over to see her sister. They are very friendly people. We did not start tonight.

Thursday, August 21st: Did not start until after breakfast. Reached the level [the ferry] about 10 o'clock. There were lots of Indians there and the men got four of them to help them. We got over the ferry about 2 o'clock; got up the hill. Found a shagnappi bag full of tent pegs. Camped on the top of the hill. We baked and went to water the cattle and there were Indians coming across the ferry, so we picked up and went up three miles.

Apparently the new settlers were somewhat suspicious of the natives!

Friday, August 22nd: Started very early. Made a good way before breakfast. Had a good many hills to climb. Camped at night by St. Laurent mission. Went to the house and got some potatoes from Father Andrews [Fr. André]. He was very kind and gave them to us for nothing. There was a thunderstorm at night.

Monday, August 25th: Started about ten o'clock today as it was raining. Got to the commencement of the settlement where we camped. Rained all morning.

Tuesday, August 26th: Started after breakfast and came through the village. Camped at noon the other side of Captain Moore's hill. Had the Captain and McKenzie to see us after dinner. Then we started and went to Captain Young's and there we had to stay as we could get no further on account of the smallpox.

Fifty-four days on the road from Winnipeg to Prince Albert — give me an airplane!

REV. DANIEL M. GORDON

In 1879 the Rev. Daniel M. Gordon (8) of Ottawa went to San Francisco by rail and then north to the Skeena River from whence he crossed northern British Columbia with Messrs. Cambie, Macleod, and Dr. G. M. Dawson, the celebrated geologist. From Edmonton he traveled east alone by way of Battleford, Carlton, Gabriel's Crossing and Humboldt. At that time Battleford had been the capital of the N.W.T. for three years. It boasted a Hudson's Bay post, a N.W.M. Police barracks, a printing office, a few shops, and several dwelling houses. At Humboldt he visited the telegraph station but found that the line was down somewhere to the east of that point. In passing through the Touchwood Hills he crossed one of the newly established Indian reserves. Here, Mr. Scott, the instructor of the Indian Farm, had a number of Indians busily engaged working the land and building barns. The chief, Day Star, was setting his tribe a good example by adopting a settled life and by farming some land. On October the seventeenth he reached the Hudson's Bay Company's trading post, the third one which was built in this area, and the one whose remains lie beside the present highway between Lestock and Punnichy. At numerous points along the route Gordon noticed that prairie fires were burning. At Fort Ellice he remarked that the post was no longer surrounded by a palisade for protection from the Indians (Fig. 37). Just another sign that the old order was changing. Also at Bird Tail Creek he learned that the Hamilton Colonization Company had secured two townships with a view to settlement. At Shoal Lake he found a Mounted Police post; at that time this place was on the western border of Manitoba. Here all the westbound travelers had their luggage examined and none was allowed to take in liquor except by special permit. At Salt Lake he fell in with some Ontario farmers who had just selected farms nearby. At the Little Saskatchewan they were visited in camp by a couple of Scotsmen, one of whom had spent some years in Ontario. Gordon asked him how long it was since he had left Scotland. "Hoo did ye ken that I cam' frae Scotland?" asked his new acquaintance in surprise! Finally on approaching Winnipeg they found that the construction of the C.P.R. west of the city had commenced, and the farmers between Portage la Prairie and Winnipeg were threshing their wheat. Winnipeg was then a lively young city of 10,000 inhabitants.

HON. J. F. BETTS

In 1879, in the month of May, a young man of twenty-five arrived in Winnipeg from Ontario. He was J. F. Betts (10), future resident of the young colony of Prince Albert and future speaker of the legislature of the Northwest Territories. For a time he took a job as cook for a group of Indian-farm instructors who were stopping at Winnipeg temporarily before going out to their posts of duty on the reserves. But soon he decided to go to the Prince Albert settlement, with an acquaintance named Gwynne, as a trader.

Accordingly, they left Winnipeg on July the first with an "outfit" of two oxen, a horse and three carts filled with provisions and groceries. They walked beside the carts the whole distance of five hundred odd miles and arrived at Prince Albert on August the eighteenth. He made his home in Prince Albert but in the following years did considerable freighting and so became very familiar with the old Trail. At one time he had a train of thirty-nine carts drawn by oxen and ponies. One man usually took charge of four carts and ponies or oxen. A cart could carry from 750 to 1200 pounds of freight, and twenty miles a day was considered good progress. It usually took from forty to fifty days to travel in this fashion from Winnipeg to Prince Albert. On one trip during a particularly wet season he says he started out over the Quill Plain at sunrise and at sunset he had not advanced his train more than a thousand yards in spite of hard work the whole day. At times these early freighters earned the five cents per pound that they charged for freighting goods from Winnipeg to Prince Albert.

According to Mr. Betts, birch wood was at a premium around Prince Albert in those days:

The birch was not very plentiful and the Indians were very jealous of what there was for making their "jumpers" [sleighs made out of rough wood]. Once Gwynne went over the river for wood and he ran into a beautiful grove of birch. He cut it all down. Then I thought of a good scheme, and that was that we could write some Christmas cards on birch bark. So we assembled around the fire and pulled a lot of the bark off and trimmed the pieces up pretty good and put "Merry Christmas" on them, and those Christmas cards went to England and Ireland and all over Canada.

FIG. 27—"The Hill of the Cross" as it appeared in September, 1954. It is now called Mount Carmel.

We are indebted to Mr. Betts for the following account of "The Hill of the Cross," which is now known as Mount Carmel (Fig. 27). This hill, three miles north of Carmel, Sask., is now crowned by a statue of Mary and the infant Jesus:

In the year 1878 a party of half-breeds were going into Winnipeg. There was a priest with the party. There was a young half-breed girl and they were going down to Winnipeg to marry her to a fellow she did not want. They found her dead in her tent. She had taken poison. There was no service over her as she was a Catholic and had committed suicide. A cross was erected on the hill. It was about 14 feet high and the cross tree would be 8 or 10 feet long. There were about 50 names carved on it with jack-knives when I saw it. The cross was made of spruce or tamarack. There was no inscription on it. The Hill of the Cross was just 12 miles on the Prince Albert side of the old telegraph station. They called it 12-mile plain. There was a bluff and the cross was on the edge of the wood. The trail ran past the foot of the hill. There was a spring right in the side of the little mountain and the spot was a great camping ground. The top of the hill would be several hundred feet above the level.

It may be noted here that the exact date when this cross was erected is a matter of uncertainty. Jarvis noted it in the spring of 1875 and Trow mentioned seeing it in 1877.

THE SURVEYORS

A most interesting episode in the history of Western Canada was the surveying of the vast territory into townships and sections so that the Hudson's Bay Company, the railway companies, and the settlers could find their lands without any trouble or confusion.

The men who carried out this huge task probably varied greatly in outlook and temperament. Those who had the vision to see something of the possibilities of the new land, and who also had the capacity to enjoy the rugged life they were called upon to endure in their daily routine, must have felt that it was a privilege, indeed, to pave the way for the settlement of

91

Fig. 28—*Well-established farm in rolling parkland. In the hollow beyond the telephone post is a "hay slough" surrounded by a ring of willow bushes.*

the rich farm (Fig. 28) and range lands stretching all the way from the Red River to the Rocky Mountains.

The general plan of the survey was very simple and clear-cut. Starting along the international boundary line in south-eastern Manitoba, the whole country was divided into town-ships six miles square, and each township was subsequently divided into thirty-six sections, one mile square, with road allowances dividing them. The sections in turn were divided into four quarters each containing 160 acres. The first strip of townships, lying east and west along the international boun-dary, were all referred to as "Township number one," and each successive strip to the north of it was numbered in numerical order. Beginning at several different meridians of longitude, the strips of townships running north and south along the west side of the meridian in question, were referred to as Range one, west of the first, second, or third meridian, as the case might be. The strips of townships to the west of it became Range two, Range three, Range four, and so on until the next meridian was reached. Stakes were placed at the northeast corner of every section and township with numbers carved on them. Thus, after the survey was completed, every individual quarter section in the surveyed portions of the Northwest had its own special numerical designation. For example, the quarter section on which the third Hudson's Bay post in the Touchwood Hills was built, was designated as follows: S.W. ¼ Section 29 - Township 27 - Range 15, west of the 2nd Meridian. The second initial meridian passed close to the east of Fort Pelly and about thirty miles west of Fort Ellice. Certain irregularities occurred here and there, because the meridian lines get closer together as they approach the North Pole, and a few of the older settlements were surveyed before the area as a whole was marked out.

One great advantage of the simple system of survey was this—by finding one of the survey posts one could easily compute how far, and in what direction, he was from any place of which he already knew the location: for example, 31-25-14 W. 2nd Mer. is nine miles N.W. of 1-25-14 W. 2nd Mer., or 12-15-10 W. 3rd Mer. is 30 miles N. and six miles E. of 12-10-11 W. 3rd Mer.

Fortunately we have available the firsthand account of Mr. A. J. Loveridge of Grenfell, Saskatchewan, of how surveying parties were organized and how they traveled to the areas assigned to them and accomplished their work.

The following extracts are taken from Mr. Loveridge's written account (16) of his own experiences:

As a youth of nineteen I was engaged with the survey party of D. C. O'Keefe, at Winnipeg in 1882. After we had loaded our outfit on a railway car we left the city early in July. Our outfit consisted of two oxen, one milch cow, four Indian ponies, two Red River carts and three other carts, a buckboard, two tents, camping and surveying equipment, provisions and baggage.

At that time the railway line ended at Oak Lake, Manitoba. There we loaded our carts and proceeded over the prairie until we reached a cart-trail leading from Fort Ellice in Manitoba to Qu'Appelle in Saskatchewan. Following this cart-trail, we touched the construction work on the main line of the Canadian Pacific Railway, at a point now called Broadview. Then we travelled north-west, and entered the Qu'Appelle Valley down the Hudson's Bay Hill, [which is north of the town of Summerberry]. We proceeded up the valley and crossed the Qu'Appelle River at a place now known as Ellisboro, where a family of half-breeds by the name of Rosette lived in a log house. They operated a raft as a ferry, and as the river was high that year and for many years after, and could not be forded, our carts, etc., were taken over on this ferry. The oxen, cow and ponies were forced to swim across.

We called at the Lebret Mission, where three French half-breeds were engaged to go with our party. They proved to be valuable helpers, and they remained with us until our work was completed. At Fort Qu'Appelle we halted for a day, and then proceeded northwards following a cart-trail for several days, and then struck across country to the south of Township 29, Range 3, west of the third meridian. We ascertained our position by the survey marks, for that country had been or was being surveyed at that time. It had taken us four weeks to reach the point where we began our work of surveying.

While travelling on the trail north of Fort Qu'Appelle, we overtook a band of freighters, who were taking loads to some of the northern trading posts, and we travelled with them for that day. I counted over ninety carts strung out, one behind the other, that day. These freighters were half-breeds, who rode ponies, and they kept the oxen and ponies hitched to the carts, on the move. They travelled about fifteen miles a day, but as we were anxious to get to our work, we pushed on faster than they. This proved to be a mistake, for we played out our oxen and ponies, before we reached our work.

The outlines of the townships were supposed to have been surveyed previously by another party. Our work was to subdivide the townships into sections and quarter sections. However, we found it necessary to outline some of the townships before we could subdivide them.

The head surveyor and the assistant used an instrument called a theodolite, which I understand is a certain type of transit. This instrument is made of brass, and is mounted on a tripod about four or four and a half feet high. It is fitted with two levels, so that it can be set quite level, and a plumb bob is used for setting the instrument over a marked spot on the ground. It is equipped with a telescope, which is hung in a frame, and which can be turned over, so that the operator can look backwards to a spot from whence he came, set the telescope in place by using clamp screws, and then turning the telescope over he can look directly ahead.

In the telescope there are two hairs or silk threads, stretched across, one running horizontal and the other vertical, so that the operator can sight an object through the telescope, at a point where the silk threads or hairs cross in the exact centre. The telescope could be turned around at any angle, and fastened in place. When we came to a lake too deep to wade through we would survey around it [see sketch].

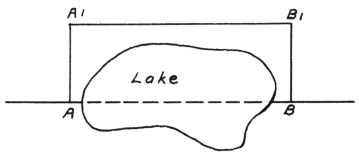

Simple method: If the necessary offset distance from the line AB was short, perpendiculars AA1=BB1 were erected to clear the lake. The line A1B1 was then chained and its length was taken as AB.

My first job at surveying was that of picket man. I carried a pole painted black and white [or it may have been white with red], about one and a half to two inches in diameter, and about seven feet long. It was iron shod at the bottom, and pointed so that it could be pushed into the ground. There was a flag at the top so that it could be seen from a distance of from one-quarter to half a mile, or perhaps even further.

I would go ahead of the surveyor, in as near as possible straight line to the highest ground or ridge. I would then hold the pole upright, and face the surveyor. He would have his instrument set, and would wave to me with his arm, either to the right or left, until I had placed the pole in exactly the right place to one inch. Then he would wave both arms downward, which indicated that I had placed the pole in the proper place. I would then make a hole in which to set another stake, for we carried several with us. This would be of the thickness of a good walking stick, and perhaps five feet long.

While I was proceeding onward to another high piece of ground, the surveyor would come to the place where I had placed the stake. He would take it out, and set his instrument directly over the hole, using a plummet, level the instrument, and sight back to the stake from where he had started. He would then turn the telescope over to the direction in which we were surveying, and again direct me, as before, on the exact line. In this way we could continue.

The two chainmen, with a sixty-six foot steel chain would follow close behind. When they had measured forty chains [or half a mile] along this line, they would mark the spot with a poplar post. This post was about three feet long, and two or three inches in diameter. It was flattened on TWO sides with an axe, and marked "¼" with a knife on one side or both sides of the post.

When the chainmen had measured another forty chains, they would set in the ground a post flattened on FOUR sides. On the south-west side of the post would be marked the numbers of the section, township, range, and meridian. For example, X XXV VII III would mean Section 10, Township 25, Range 7, West of the third meridian. In this way we would survey from the south line of a township, northwards to the northern line of a township. Only the east and north sides of the section were marked with posts, so that in later years when the road allowances were marked out, the measurements were made from these posts. However, when we made correction lines, two rows of posts were required, on each side of the road allowance.

When we reached the "top" or northern part of the township, we seldom hit the post or mound, as outlined by the township surveyors, for we might be east or west of it by many yards. If this were the case, a man would be sent back, perhaps for one or two miles, to move the posts, either to the east or west as the case might be, and as figured out by the surveyor. The first post would be moved a certain distance, the second post a shorter distance, and so on. This accounts for the fact that some roads are not straight.

After the lines had been corrected, a man or perhaps two men, called the "mound-builders" would build mounds around the posts. They would use a sharp spade, and build the mound about two and a half feet square, and about eighteen inches high, with the dirt taken out of four square holes of a certain size. The township corners had larger mounds than those used for marking the sections, and we used an iron stake, about one inch thick, and we marked the Roman numerals on, with a cold chisel.

Sometimes we found that the section posts should be located in a slough, lake, or creek. If such were the case, we would place the post on higher ground close by, and measure the distance from the post to the place where the post should have been, and make the necessary notation in our record book. This post would be marked differently, and the mound would be round with a ditch around it.

After working for several days as a picket man, my job was changed to that of head chainman. The name "head chainman" may seem confusing for I was at the rear end of the chain. I had a half-breed to pull the chain. He would carry ten steel pins, made of heavy stiff wire, about eighteen inches long. At the top of the pin there was a round loop, and the bottom of the pin was sharpened, so that it could be pushed into the ground. When the chain was pulled to its full length along the line, straight, and just tight enough, I would say "right" or "down." The other man would push the pin into the ground, and go on, as before, to measure another chain's length. In this way we continued until all ten pins had been set in the ground. I would then pick up the pins, and count them, and give them to the man pulling the chain.

I found this work as head chainman to be very exacting. We chained long stretches, and as I have said, in addition to outlining the sections we also outlined some townships. We put in correction lines, which were very difficult, and I found it necessary to keep a level head, in order that the measurements would be correct, and the posts properly marked.

As head chainman I carried a book in which to make records. For every ten chains measured, I would record in the book "1 talley". When four talleys were recorded [being one-half mile] a stake or post would be set in the ground. At the proper places we allowed

97

one chain for the road allowance. I also recorded in the book notes regarding the type of country, whether flat or undulating, hilly or otherwise, scrubby, bluffy, stoney, sloughy, the kind of soil, stoney, alkaline, etc. When we came to a fair-sized lake, I would mark in the book the measurement to the edge of the lake, from the last post, the width of the lake, and draw a sketch of the shape, etc. On Sundays while in camp, I would carefully copy these notes and records into a much better book.

We waded through, and chained all sloughs, provided the water did not come up to our shoulders. At such times I carried my notebook in my cap, which was a tam o'shanter. Where there was little or no grass we called them lakes. If these sloughs or lakes were too deep to wade through we would measure around them and this work took a long time. Sometimes we would make a triangulation [see sketch].

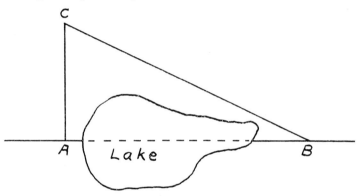

The angle at A was 90°, AC and BC were measured. Knowing the length of AC and BC, the length AB could be computed.

In the fall we worked until dark, and then made our way back some miles to the camp. Often we walked but sometimes we rode in a Red River cart. When it was clear we guided ourselves by the stars, until we sighted the lighted cook tent, or the camp fire. When it was overcast or foggy, and we could see no stars, we would note the direction of the wind, and travel accordingly.

The half-breeds could find their way over these miles of prairie much better than we white men, for we had little sense of direction, and soon became lost. I will say that I considered myself pretty good at finding my directions. These half-breeds were also very good at telling the time by the sun.

During the summer the only wild life we saw were some jumping deer, wolves, foxes and prairie chicken, and plenty of gophers and ducks. I think that we outlined and subdivided fourteen townships. We finished our work on November 10, and commenced our return journey across the ninety miles of plains. We followed a cart-trail from the Whitecap Indian Reserve, which was a few miles north of where we had finished our survey; and then we went on to the Touchwood Hills Trading Post, which we reached after travelling about five days. From this trading post we proceeded to Fort Qu'Appelle, where our party disbanded. During the summer the railway had been extended, so we took a stage to Qu'Appelle station, and then travelled by train back to Winnipeg, arriving there about the 20th of November. One of the first things we did was to have a good clean-up, a shave, and a hair-cut, for we had let our beards grow, and we certainly looked like wild men.

THE SURVEY REPORTS

In 1886 the Department of the Interior at Ottawa issued a publication entitled *Descriptions of the Townships of the Northwest Territories, Dominion of Canada, Between the Second and Third Initial Meridian* (46). In it are to be found reports sent in by the men in charge of the surveying parties who marked out the virgin prairies and woodlands of southeastern Saskatchewan into townships, sections, and quarter sections. Evidently the townships were blocked out first and a year or two later another party marked out the smaller units within each township. These reports described the topography of the land, and its suitability for farming purposes, rating it as first, second, or third class land. The reports also mentioned the presence of lakes, streams, or trails of importance. The Carlton Trail was referred to repeatedly, but received quite a variety of designations, such as "the main trail from Fort Ellice to Edmonton," "the Winnipeg and Battleford trail," "the trail from Fort Ellice to Touchwood Hills," "the Prince Albert

99

trail," and "the main cart trail, to and from Carlton, Battleford, and Fort Ellice." The point is this: The famous prairie highway, which had connected Fort Garry, Fort Carlton, and Edmonton for a period of nearly forty years did not have any commonly accepted name among these various survey parties, and few of the leaders seemed to know just where it led. The following are a few examples of the many entries referring to the Carlton Trail to be found in the surveyors' reports:

Township 23, Range 8 (near Fenwood, Sask.)—"There is a cart trail leading from Fort Ellice to Touchwood that crosses it from the south-east to the north-west corner." L. E. Le Moine, 1882.

Township 25, Range 10 (near Hubbard)—"The Saskatchewan trail crosses Section 18." J. L. Reid, 1882.

Township 26, Range 13 (near Kelliher)—"The Winnipeg and Battleford trail crosses Section 13." W. Ogilvie, 1880.

The author saw the Old Trail near this place in 1908. It passed just to the southwest of Birch Lake and the site of the present town of Kelliher, and about eight miles northeast of our homestead. It had already fallen into disuse but its ruts were still quite distinct. It consisted of six or eight wheel tracks, winding in unison between the numerous bluffs and sloughs, and avoiding soft spots and steep hillsides as much as possible.

Township 28, Range 16—"The main trail from Ellice to Edmonton crosses Section 19". E. Deville, 1880. "The telegraph line and trail to the north-west cross the township diagonally." J. L. Reid, 1880-1881.

This is the township in which the telegraph station at Kutawa and the old Indian Agency were located.

Township 30, Range 18—"A small creek, 4 feet wide, 12 inches deep, good water, swift current, and a cart trail from Touchwood Hills to Prince Albert, cross Section 30. An old cart trail and the telegraph line from Touchwood Hills to Prince Albert, and a ravine 20 feet deep, cross Section 31." A. C. Talbot, 1883.

Township 31, Range 18—"The old cart trail from Touchwood Post to Battleford and Prince Albert passes through the south-west corner of Section 6." A. O. Wheeler, 1884.

These last statements show that the trail followed alternate routes at certain places. The two just mentioned lie along the present Highway No. 6 at points about ten and eleven miles south of the town of Dafoe.

The following is the report of the survey party that outlined the township on which the telegraph station of Humboldt stood in 1883:

Township 37, Range 23—"Outlines: West—broken, open, rolling prairie. Numerous small marshes were crossed. Subsoils, sand, sandy clay, clay and yellow clay; class 2. A ridge and a coulee cross Section 6. The cart trail from Touchwood to Prince Albert, and the telegraph line, cross the township. East—rolling to level prairie, half covered with willow and young poplar; there is also a large quantity of small, dry poplar. Soil, 4 inches deep, on clay, yellow clay, sand and sandy clay subsoils; class 2. Sections 25 and 36 are rolling, open prairie." A. C. Talbot, 1883.

At the time these reports were compiled, the townships along the Carlton Trail from the Quill Plains to the vicinity of the present town of Wakaw had not been subdivided, and those in charge of the survey parties which outlined the townships made very few references to the Carlton Trail. However, a map of the whole region was included with the report, and this shows the route followed by the trail, all the way from the point at which the trail crossed Big Cut Arm Creek (near Fort Ellice) to Batoche and Gabriel's Crossing.

The routes followed by the trail and the telegraph line are shown in greater detail on large-scale sectional maps of the

101

FIG. 29—*The old stone church at Wishart, Sask., built in 1888. It was quite near Kutawa and the Carlton Trail northeast of Punnichy.*

Touchwood, Humboldt, and Prince Albert South districts. These were published in 1914 and 1916. According to these maps, Kutawa (Fig. 29) was on the N.E. $\frac{1}{4}$ of 10-28-16, W. 2nd Meridian. The Humboldt telegraph station (original site) was between the N.W. $\frac{1}{4}$ of Section 9 and the N.E. $\frac{1}{4}$ of Section 8-37-23, but it was subsequently moved to the N.E. $\frac{1}{4}$ of 23-36-23. The Hoodoo stage coach station was about the middle of Township 41, Range 25.

EDWARD FIELD

An Englishman by the name of Edward Field came to the Red River Settlement in August, 1867. For a time he freighted supplies from Winnipeg to Fort Ellice and the Touchwood Hills post. After spending about nine years on various undertakings, such as fur trading and freighting, he homesteaded at Big Point on the west shore of Lake Manitoba. The following account tells in his own words how he and his family migrated to the

Shell River district in what is now western Manitoba. In this trek he followed the northern branch of the Carlton Trail from Westbourne to Shoal Lake, where the Fort Pelly Trail branched off to the northwest:

> In 1880 the water of Lake Manitoba rose so high that it came into my stable, so I thought it time to leave. I had already received the patent for my place, but under the circumstances was allowed to homestead again. Therefore I pulled out once more, but it was no little undertaking. We had four children, one three months old, 30 oxen and carts, and 30 head of cattle, not to mention household effects. The Shell River country, now Russell, was my destination, there were some 250 miles of bad roads, rivers and creeks to cross, and with cows calving and straying, sticking in mud holes, fighting mosquitoes, and numerous other difficulties, it was six weeks ere we reached the spot where Russell now stands, then called the Shell River district. Prairie City, or Tanners Crossing, now Minnedosa, was our nearest town 100 miles off. As we passed, the C.P.R. engineers were surveying their main line to run through Minnedosa, but of course the line was taken further south. I mention the foregoing to show the difficulties and the troubles one had to contend with in those days locating a new home, compared with the present day immigrant.

In 1892 Mr. Field and his family moved to the shore of Fishing Lake, near the place where Wadena now stands. Here he traded with the Indians and built up a horse and cattle ranch. As the district became settled he took his place as one of the leaders in the new community and served as justice of the peace and secretary of his local improvement district for many years.

LORD LORNE, GOVERNOR GENERAL OF CANADA

In the summer of 1881 Lord Lorne, then Governor General of Canada, made a tour through Manitoba and the Northwest Territories. Mr. W. H. Williams, a special correspondent of the Toronto *Globe,* was sent out West to accompany the Governor General's party and report matters of interest in connection with the trip to his paper (48). We will concern ourselves with the portion of his trip during which they followed the Carlton Trail.

Starting out from Winnipeg on August the eighth, they traveled by train until they reached the end of the track, then at a point about thirty-five miles west of Portage la Prairie. On the way they saw a herd of domesticated buffalo feeding near the railway just east of Stony Mountain. They were the property of the warden of the penitentiary. At Portage la Prairie a large crowd of whites and Indians was gathered to welcome Lord Lorne. The Sioux and Ojibway remained apart in two separate bands as they apparently were not on very friendly terms.

At the end of the steel they were met by an outfit in charge of a detachment of Mounted Police under the command of Colonel Herchmer. The Mounties made a very fine showing in their bright uniforms, and the horses were fine-looking animals decked out in attractive harness. Enough carriages and baggage wagons were provided to carry the Governor General's party, but Mr. Williams was traveling with his own equipment: a buckboard and a team of horses, with a half-breed to help look after the horses and do the cooking. Between Portage la Prairie and Fort Ellice the vice-regal party made several stops at embryonic towns, where they were accorded rude but enthusiastic receptions. At Fort Ellice, Lord Lorne was entertained at the Hudson's Bay post by Archie McDonald. That summer, river steamers were plying between this post and Fort Garry via the Assiniboine River. About 500 Indians were gathered at the post to see the Queen's representative and he held a pow-wow with their chiefs. The Indians were dressed in their picturesque native costumes.

The Governor General next visited Fort Qu'Appelle, but Mr. Williams' buckboard broke down and he did not succeed in catching up with the party until it was past the Touchwood

Hills on its way to Carlton. His account of his reception on rejoining the party is as follows:

I had now gone ten miles north and west on the Edmonton [Carlton] trail before I had the satisfaction of seeing His Excellency's camp pitched just to the left of the trail. I had been out of sight of it for just one week, and doing all in my power to reach it. I met with the most cordial and hearty reception on reaching the camp, and my mares had hardly come to a standstill before some of the Mounted Police Force were unharnessing them, while others were unloading the wagon and pitching my tent. I had barely set foot upon the ground when I was cordially welcomed back to camp by Colonel DeWinton, who brought a request from His Excellency that I should dine with him. It is needless to say that such a cordial welcome was grateful this evening, after what has been to me unquestionably a very hard and perplexing week's work. According to his custom His Excellency had camped on Saturday night to remain without stirring further till Monday morning, and it was in this Sunday camp that I overtook the vice-regal party. The only events of any account which had taken place in Lord Lorne's progress during the past week were the loss of some few horses and the loss of a finger by Constable Leamy of the Mounted Police. A wagon had stuck in a mudhole, and he was adjusting a rope with which it was to be pulled out, when the horses started up suddenly and his finger was caught in a bit of rope and was crushed so hopelessly that Dr. Sewell found it necessary to amputate it at the second joint.

Upon reaching the South Saskatchewan River at Gabriel's Crossing, Mr. Williams crossed over and drove ahead to Carlton, but the Governor General's party went north about six miles and crossed at Batoche:

Less than half hour after my arrival here an escort of Mounted Police came cantering down to the Fort, quickly followed by ambulances containing His Excellency and suite, and these in turn by the remainder of the outfit. I must admit that I was not a little surprised, not merely with the fact that Colonel Herchmer and his men had succeeded with a single scow in bringing over a broad, swift river in five hours an outfit consisting of twenty loaded ambulances, baggage wagons and other vehicles, and no less than eighty-one horses, but after this severe task, and after

105

the officers and men of the force had been steadily engaged in such a long and arduous march through the wilderness, they should be able to ride into the fort clean, pipe-clayed, and in all respects as though they were just out of their barracks, seemed well nigh incredible.

Fort Carlton at that time was still in the hands of the Hudson's Bay Company. During his brief stay there, Lord Lorne was the guest of Mr. Lawrence Clark, chief factor of the Carlton District. An assemblage of chiefs and head men met the Governor General at this place. During the powwow, Mistawasis, an old and celebrated Cree chief, spoke as follows:

I was glad that God has permitted me to meet the Governor. I feel flattered that it was a Governor who put this medal on my neck. I did not put it on myself. We are the children of the Great Mother, and we wish that through her representative, our brother-in-law, she would listen for a little while to our complaints and sympathize with our sufferings. I have no great complaints to make, but I wish to make just a few remarks concerning our property. The kindness that has been shown us is great, but in our eyes it is not quite enough to put us on our feet. In days gone by the buffalo was our wealth and our strength, but he has left us. In those days we used the horse to chase the buffalo, and when the buffalo left us we thought we might use the horse to follow after other game but we have lost many of our ponies with the mange and we have had to sell others, and when I look around me and see that the buffaloes are gone and that our ponies are no longer left to us, I think I and my people are poor indeed. The white man knows whence his strength comes and we know where we require more strength. The strength to harvest crops is in animals and in implements, and we have not enough of these. If our crops should be enough to keep us alive we would not have the means with which to harvest them. We would very much like more working cattle and more farming implements. I would beg also that if possible a grist mill should be put up somewhere within our reach, so that we can have our wheat ground into flour and our other crops ground. I do not speak for myself but those poor people behind me. I am very thankful that I am able to see the Governor General in my old days. He has come just in time that I may see him before I die. Many a time have I been in terrible

106

straits for food for myself and my people, but I have never been angry about it, for I knew the Indian agent was a good friend to us, and that he always acted on the instructions left for him, which he was bound to obey. Often have I been sorely perplexed and miserable at seeing my people starving and shrunken in flesh until they were so weak that with the first cold striking them they would fall off their feet and then nothing would save them. We want teachers to instruct and educate our children; we want guns and traps and nets to help us to get ready for winter. We try to do all that the farm instructor has told us, and we are doing the best we can, but, as I said before, we want farming implements. I do not speak for myself, as I am getting old, but I speak for my people and for my children and grandchildren, who must starve if they do not receive the help they so much need.

Truly a forceful exposition of the Indian's position at that time, and an eloquent plea for help of the proper kind from the race which had bought the Indian's country for a mere pittance. Mr. Williams described the occasion:

His Excellency told them in reply that the Great Mother had many white children who were very poor, some of whom thought she was giving to the red men more than their share. She would gladly give them all that they needed, but she had so many poor children who needed assistance that she could not always do as much for them as she would wish to. He had noticed, however, that some of their requests contained certain practical suggestions, and he would endeavour to see if some assistance could not be given them in that particular direction. His Excellency then presented Big Child [Mistawasis] and Star Blanket with beautiful silver medals with medallion busts of the princess and himself. One of the richest and most gorgeous Indian dresses I have ever seen was worn by the great Sioux chief, White Cap. He wore a beautiful snow-white tunic of fine caribou skin, richly ornamented with porcupine quills, coloured silk, and bead work. From his shoulders hung some twenty or thirty scalps taken in the horrible Minnesota massacre.

From Carlton the Governor General's party went to the Prince Albert settlement on the steamer *Northcote,* and later took a boat trip up the river to Battleford on the steamer *Lily.* Then they traveled across country to Calgary, and on the way

107

saw a herd of thirteen buffalo bulls of which they killed several. At the Blackfoot Crossing of the Bow River they found 2,000 Blackfoot encamped and near them a smaller encampment of Sarcee. Lord Lorne held a confab with their chiefs, headed by Crowfoot. They visited Calgary and Fort Macleod and then the vice-regal party proceeded home by Fort Benton and other points in the United States, but Mr. Williams and his half-breed helper returned via Edmonton, Battleford, Touchwood Hills and Fort Ellice.

They left Calgary on October the fifth and were unfortunate in having an unusually wet and cold autumn in which to make the return trip. When they reached Clark's Crossing on November the eleventh, "lily pads" of ice were floating down on the rapid current and it was with some difficulty that they succeeded in persuading the ferry man to attempt to ferry them over. However, they got everything across by dint of much exertion, but immediately the weather turned extremely cold and stormy. We will let Mr. Williams tell what camping in such weather was like, at a spot about twenty miles east of Clark's Crossing:

It was almost impossible for one who has not experienced a similar situation to fully comprehend our utterly dismal condition tonight. The cold is so intense that our mercury thermometers are of no use, and in addition to this a cutting wind from the north-east is howling hungrily over this great, shroud-like, treeless waste, so that it is with difficulty that we pitched our tents. The heavy Hudson Bay blankets have been damp with frost for weeks, and tonight as they were unfolded they were frozen stiff, almost as stiff as the frozen tents themselves. Let one who likes sleeping in a warm room judge how much comfort he could derive from shovelling the snow from off the rough, frozen ground, pitching a tent in a gale of wind with the temperature thirty-five or forty below zero, and after a half-thawed supper, wrapping himself in damp, frozen blankets, and spending the night in sleeping snatches of an hour at a time, and the intervals in speculating as to whether he will be frost-bitten or not. Tonight is perhaps an exceptionally bad one, but it promises to be only a little worse than many others already experienced on this trip.

Finally, he and a number of fellow travelers changed their wagons for jumpers at the Touchwood Post and from thence made their way to the end of the railway at Brandon. Mr. Williams parted with his faithful ponies with keen regret and returned to the East over the new, partially completed transcontinental railway.

REV. ANDREW BAIRD

Late in August of 1881, not long after the Governor General departed on his tour of the Territories, an energetic young Presbyterian minister arrived in Winnipeg to begin the 900-mile trek to Edmonton where he was to serve as a pioneer missionary. The call had come to him from his church in May of that year while he was studying theology in Germany. Wishing to ascertain where Edmonton was, he had hunted up an atlas of North America and had been astonished to find that the region in which Edmonton should have appeared was marked "unexplored territory"!

Returning to Canada during the summer, Mr. Baird was ordained in the church at his native town of Motherwell in Ontario and shortly after left for Winnipeg, eager to undertake his new mission. Here he spent some time as a guest of Professor Thomas Hart of Manitoba College while he completed preparations for the long journey. As the season for such travel was getting late, he was unable to find a traveling companion, so he set off alone.

The Rev. Andrew Baird's "outfit" consisted of a horse, which rejoiced in the name of Shaganappi, a buckboard, a single harness and tethering rope for the horse, a tent, a blanket, and a buffalo robe, a few cooking utensils and some bacon, hard tack and other provisions.

Mr. Baird's journey over the Carlton Trail was an eventful one and he encountered many interesting people. First of all

FIG. 30—*First telegraph office in the Northwest Territories, at Humboldt.*

he met the Rev. Hugh McKellar, who was stationed at that time at High Bluff near Portage la Prairie. This gentleman had already served as a missionary in the Indian mission at Prince Albert from 1874 to 1876, taking charge of that mission after its founder, the Rev. James Nisbet, was retired. In 1881, Reverend McKellar was ministering to a congregation in a comparatively well-settled part of Manitoba. We have no details of the first meeting of these two pioneer ministers, but probably the elder had a lot of useful information to give the younger concerning the people and conditions in the new land.

From Portage la Prairie Mr. Baird proceeded by the northern branch of the Carlton Trail. At Minnedosa he visited the Rev. James Robertson, supervisor of missions for the Presbyterian Church in the West. After more than a week's travel he crossed the bridge over the Assiniboine River and climbed the steep road to Fort Ellice. He carried a letter of introduction from Reverend Robertson to Archibald McDonald, the factor at the post, but this was not necessary to secure an enthusiastic welcome. It was Saturday night and Mr. McDonald and his

110

wife extended a cordial invitation to the young minister to stay over Sunday. "It is time out of mind," the factor said, "since we have had a religious service and now that we have a resident clergyman we will have two services tomorrow."

At Fort Ellice Mr. Baird met several other interesting individuals. These included W. F. King, a land surveyor for the Dominion Government and a former university acquaintance of Mr. Baird's, John Calder, the clerk of the fort, and Major Boulton of Russell, Manitoba, who was electioneering at the time as a candidate for a seat in the legislature of the province of Manitoba. His sparsely inhabited constituency had just been formed along the western border of the only Prairie Province then in existence. Major Boulton subsequently organized and led "Boulton's Mounted Infantry" during the 1885 Rebellion.

Mr. Baird spent a long and pleasant evening with his new acquaintances. In his own words:

> We sat around the open fire that Saturday evening, the blaze from the dry poplar logs flaming up the wide chimney, and we talked and talked. When the evening was over, Mrs. McDonald, tallow candle in hand, escorted me to my room. She stopped impressively at the door and said, "The last man who slept in that bed was the Marquis of Lorne." The Marquis was then the Governor General of Canada, and had signalized his term of office by visiting Manitoba, penetrating to the Western Plains and shooting a buffalo.

The next day, Sunday, September the eighteenth, the young minister held two services in a house beside the fort. Bright and early Monday morning he set out for Fort Qu'Appelle, on the trail that led along the south side of the Qu'Appelle Valley, just far enough back from its southern rim to avoid most of the sharp ravines that lead into the valley every few miles. He had company for a time, as the mailman and a young storekeeper named Fish, who was going to Prince Albert, were traveling the same way. Everything went as planned the first day and the minister spent his first night under canvas and slept soundly. His brief entry in his diary for that day runs: "Started off with Mr. Fish and the mail—got on swimmingly. My first day of real life on the plains." The pun comes as a surprise from a staid young cleric.

At the end of the second day, while going down a steep hill, one of the wheels of Mr. Baird's buckboard got badly "dished" and in addition the front axle was bent. So the next morning the damaged wheel was patched up with sticks extending from rim to rim, and leaving his heavy trunk behind to take some of the strain off the damaged wheel and axle, he set out for the blacksmith's shop at Fort Qu'Appelle, a distance of about sixty miles, to have his vehicle repaired. Regarding this stage of his journey, he wrote:

> With my lightened buckboard I was able still to drive fast enough to keep up with the teams and that night, after crossing the Qu'Appelle by a ford, we stayed in the house of a Scotch half-breed named Roderick Ross. By special permission we were allowed to bring in our buffalo robes and blankets and sleep on the floor. I never before ate anything like the things I got that time...

On Thursday they continued their journey along the valley and arrived at Fort Qu'Appelle about two o'clock in the afternoon. The place then consisted of the Hudson's Bay post, the Mounted Police barracks, a store, and three houses occupied by the Indian agent, the commander in charge of the Mounted Police, and a married member of the Force. The policeman who usually did the blacksmithing around the place was ill and could not attend to the ailing buckboard, but a good-natured Scotsman, by the name of James Sutherland, who was also saddler to the Force, straightened the bent axle. However, the dished wheel could not be properly repaired and was left to function in its patched-up condition throughout the rest of the trip.

The missionary then returned alone for his trunk and other baggage. On Friday evening he had the good fortune to fall in with a couple of land seekers, by the names of Holmes and Mickle, with whom he camped for the night. The next day he recovered his trunk and returned as far as the Qu'Appelle River crossing, northwest of where Summerberry now stands. In crossing the river the following morning he had to take his buckboard apart and ferry it and his baggage over in intsallments on a raft. When he undertook to get his horse across he nearly lost her in the muddy-bottomed river. Finally he arrived back at Fort Qu'Appelle where he spent the evening with W. J. McLean, the man in charge of the Hudson's Bay post.

Monday was spent in getting the bent axle fixed more securely, laying in additional supplies, and giving Shaganappi her Sabbath rest which she had missed the previous day. She also received a second-hand oilcloth cover, as a present from James Sutherland, to protect her from cold winds and rain. On Tuesday morning Mr. Baird left for the Touchwood Hills in company with several teamsters who were making the fifty-mile journey to secure poplar building logs to be used in constructing an addition to the police barracks at Fort Qu'Appelle. As they left the valley a flurry of snow served warning that the Western winter was approaching. They took the left branch of the Touchwood Trail that passed to the west of the Little Touchwood Hills. At the end of the first day he and the teamsters camped a few miles short of the Anglican mission on the Gordon Indian reserve.

The next morning Mr. Baird said good-bye to his teamster friends and proceeded alone. In the evening he was pleased to find the land seekers, Holmes and Mickle, camped beside the trail on the edge of the Quill Plains. They were now on their way to Prince Albert.

The young minister did not spend a very comfortable night, for he unsuspectingly took a drink of alkaline water and it made him rather ill. It rained all night, and next day's trip across the saline plain was not a pleasant experience. Once, his companions' wagon got stuck in a mudhole and they had to jump out into the cold mud and water, unload their baggage and carry it to firm ground, hitch their ponies to the end of the wagon tongue and heave on the wheels with their shoulders to get the heavy vehicle out of the hole. However, they crossed the plain, which he stated was twenty-three miles wide, and traveled another five miles before camping for the night.

It was still drizzling when they awoke on Friday morning, but Mr. Baird decided to push on and leave the others to follow at their leisure. About the middle of the afternoon he arrived at Humboldt, a telegraph station on the long line from Selkirk to Edmonton. His brief visit with the Weldons, who were in charge of this station, was one of the bright spots of the journey. He wrote:

> The people here — Presbyterians from the North of Ireland — were very glad to see me. The lady of the house — telegraph operator — baked a couple of big bannocks for me to take with me, when they found that I was out of bread, and I was invited to stay for tea which was got ready in the middle of the afternoon.

His comment was but another tribute, to come down to us, to the hospitality of George Weldon and his wife. Unfortunately, the weather was not in such a hospitable mood. Soon after Mr. Baird left Humboldt it commenced to rain again, and in the morning the whole countryside was covered with a blanket of snow an inch and a half thick. Shaganappi was glad of her oil-cloth blanket that morning! This was the first day of October.

Crossing the South Saskatchewan River by Batoche's Ferry, Mr. Baird reached Duck Lake on Sunday. He was able to find stable room for his horse and he made camp in time to enjoy a good Sabbath rest. Here he met Father André, the local Roman Catholic priest.

Two incidents of special interest occurred during Mr. Baird's two-day stop at Duck Lake. He went to Stobart and Eden's store and wrote a long letter to his sister Jeannie, at home in Ontario. It is from a copy of this letter that much of the detail concerning this trip has been derived. Included in the letter was the following description of his daily routine:

I am sure that you would like to have a description of a specimen day's camping just to let you see how I get along. Well, I usually get up about 5:30, put on the few clothes that I have taken off the night before — these frosty nights I don't take off many — rush out and feed my horse her oats — come back and get a cold breakfast, usually bread and butter with syrup or anything that is left over from the night before (when I am alone I never light a fire in the morning), roll up my tent and bedding, pack my buckboard, harness my horse, and start. I drive usually till about 12, then take an hour and a half for dinner. If the weather is good I sometimes kindle a fire but not usually. My dinner will then be canned beef or salmon, bread and perhaps canned tomatoes or apples. In the evening my cooking talent is to be seen. After my horse is picketed, the fire is kindled and while it is burning up, the tent is pitched — not a very easy thing at first to do alone but I can manage it nicely now— indeed, I can grease my buckboard now almost as quickly as with somebody to help me. Then as soon as the fire is hot I have the water ready and make my tea or porridge or fry my bacon as the case may be. Some of these days I am going to try to make bannocks and some other devices in the way of higher cooking but the trouble now is that I have not time. Before the cooking and the supper are half over — for they often go on at the same time — it is quite dark, and by the fitful light from the dying embers of my fire I spread my blankets and turn in. I have a bit of candle but it is only now and then that I light it — when I want to read a little, for instance.

The other item of interest was the threshing of a fresh supply of oats for his horse. A field of oats nearby was in stook but none of it had been threshed, so the young minister obtained permission to thresh out a bushel or two to take with him. In order to do this he took his oilcloth horse-cover to the field and laid it on the ground for a threshing floor. Then, laying the sheaves on the cover, he beat out the grain with a stick. Evidently, from the wording of his description of the chore, he considered it a rather undignified task for an ordained minister!

115

On Tuesday, Mr. Baird traveled on to Fort Carlton and then turned south on an old buffalo-hunting trail that led past the Elbow of the North Saskatchewan River and out on the plains along the Eagle Hill Creek. At this period it seems to have been customary to take the round-about route up the right bank of the river from Fort Carlton to Battleford, rather than to ferry across it and take the shorter direct route past Redberry Lake. It was on this particular portion of his long trail that tragedy struck with shocking suddenness. His energetic and faithful Shaganappi, who could travel forty miles a day with ease, was allowed to eat too many of the incompletely matured oats, which her master had laboriously procured for her at Duck Lake, and she took colic and died. This necessitated a return to Fort Carlton on foot, followed by a drive back to Duck Lake with John Daniel to obtain another horse.

Mr. Baird purchased an Indian pony from Stobart and Eden for seventy-five dollars. The purchase had to be made on time, for the minister was not provided with sufficient funds to meet such a large and unexpected expense and still remain solvent for the balance of the trip. The little cayuse had not the strength and vigor of the late lamented Shaganappi, and the traveler found that he could make better progress if he walked or trotted alongside his pony. Consequently most of the remaining 400 miles of his journey was made on foot. That evening Mr. Baird returned to Fort Carlton with his new horse and spent the night at the Fort.

The river steamer *Lily* stopped at Fort Carlton the next day on its way from Battleford to Prince Albert. Lieutenant Governor Laird was a passenger on the boat and Mr. Baird had a very pleasant visit with him. He learned that the Lieutenant Governor was an ardent Presbyterian from Prince Edward Island and that he was very much interested in learning Hebrew so that he could read the Bible in what he considered to be the original tongue. Here for a time, and later at home in Battleford, His Excellency obtained some coaching in that language from the young university graduate. In spite of this interesting interlude, Mr. Baird did not forget that he still had 400 miles to go, so he set off again before evening and camped that night at Six Mile Creek.

The next day Mr. Baird had an exasperating and exhausting adventure with his new horse. At noon, when he took the animal to water, he found the margin of the slough very muddy so he threw the tethering rope over the pony's back and allowed him to wade in and help himself to a drink. When the pony came out of the slough he eluded his master and made a dash for freedom. For hours the worried traveler pursued the skittish creature. Every time he attempted to approach the brute it would trot away for a short distance and then start feeding on the prairie grass again when it felt safely out of reach. Once, during the early part of the chase, Mr. Baird succeeded in seizing the long tethering rope, but the horse kicked up its heels and dashed away, pulling the rope through the man's hand so fast that it burnt the skin off his palm. The wound healed in time, but it left a scar on his hand for the rest of his life. Finally Mr. Baird recaptured the beast but was faced with a new problem. He had shed his vest during the chase and now had to find it; not that the vest itself was indispensable, but the owner's good watch was in it and he could not face the prospect of traveling on without it.

The search for the garment took another hour or two, but at last camp was broken, the refractory pony hitched to the buckboard, and the exhausted man continued on his way, thankful that he was not obliged to walk back to Fort Carlton again for another horse.

After some disagreeable travel on a wet and slippery trail, Mr. Baird reached Battleford, the capital of the Northwest Territories, about mid-afternoon on Tuesday, October the eleventh. Here he was hospitably received by the Rev. T. A.

117

Clarke, a missionary to the Indians in the neighborhood. As the weather continued cold and stormy for several days, Mr. Baird remained here for nearly a week waiting for milder weather and dry roads. He obtained a much-needed rest and spent a leisurely period reading, visiting new acquaintances and teaching Hebrew to the Lieutenant Governor. Among the people of note in the little town, he met Lt. Col. Herchmer and Captain Antrobus of the North West Mounted Police, William McKay of the Hudson's Bay Company, and Mr. Laurie, the editor of the *Saskatchewan Herald*. True to form, his pony broke loose and got away for a time, but was recovered by Johnnie Saskatchewan, a local celebrity of mixed blood.

On October the eighteenth, he finally set out again, this time in company with Mr. Charles Whitford, whom he described as a very pleasant traveling companion. The leaves had fallen and there was a decided chill in the air even in the daytime and at night a fringe of ice formed around the sloughs. The travelers took the direct route west, which ran north of Beaverhill Lake and crossed the river at Fort Saskatchewan. A few days later a party including the Rev. Henry Steinhauer, a Methodist missionary from Whitefish Lake, caught up to them and traveled with them for the next two days. At the end of that time, Messrs. Whitford and Steinhauer turned off on another trail leading northward to their mission and Mr. Baird pursued his journey alone.

In his writing Reverend Baird emphasized the extreme loneliness of this stage of the trip. In a letter to the Rev. Hugh McKellar in later years, he said:

During this period I was for four days without seeing a mortal, putting up my tent each evening, tethering my horse, cooking my supper, and sleeping with the howling of wolves as a lullaby.

In a letter to his church magazine, *The Canada Presbyterian*, written just after his arrival in Edmonton, he said:

This loneliness was absolute. No one can understand how absolute it was but those who have seen a prairie, who know what solemn feelings its far-reaching monotonous waves inspire, and who know with what a melancholy "sough" the wind sighs among its long dry grass at night.

With reference to the "lullaby" of the wolves, besides the fearsome yelping and howling of small bands of coyotes, it is quite possible that the deeper and more sinister tones of the timber wolves could be heard in those days. A few years before this they had roamed the Prairies in large numbers, feeding upon weaklings of the buffalo herds and feasting on the remains of the slaughtered animals after each buffalo hunt. After living all his previous life in populous centers, the stark contrast must have seemed overpowering to the lonely young traveler.

Mr. Baird's last adventure before reaching Edmonton occurred where the trail crossed the Beaver River. The stream was not very wide but it was deep and its current was swift. Spanning it was a crude swinging foot-bridge. A small Indian encampment stood nearby but all the braves were away hunting. However, the squaws kindly helped the minister take his buckboard apart and carry it over the narrow bridge in pieces along with the harness. They then reassembled the vehicle on the far side of the stream. Next, the squaws forced the horse to swim across the creek, while Mr. Baird walked over the bridge, high and dry, controlling the animal with the long tethering rope. Soon the horse was harnessed and hitched to the buckboard again and the intrepid traveler set out on the last lap of his journey.

Mr. Baird arrived at Edmonton on October the thirty-first, forty-nine days after he had set out from Winnipeg, and he received a very warm welcome from the people of the small town and trading post. During that winter he lived for some time at the house of Chief Factor Richard Hardisty and his wife, who was the daughter of the Methodist missionary George McDougall. His long, lonely journey over the Carlton Trail was one of the most memorable recorded.

SENATOR T. O. DAVIS

In 1880, among the settlers who came into the Prince Albert district over the Carlton Trail from Winnipeg was the late Senator T. O. Davis and his brother (10). They brought with them five carts and wagons loaded with merchandise and drawn by oxen. They left Winnipeg early in September. On the first leg of the trip, they experienced the usual difficulties negotiating the mudholes, having to unload and reload their carts many times. They traveled for a while with a half-breed family which was on its way to Batoche to settle in a new home. One of the half-breed's cows not only drew a cart but also supplied the party with milk! Evidently it was a wet fall and the streams they had to cross were greatly swollen. It took them a whole day to get across one of these on the Pheasant Plains. At one point they met Charles Nolin, former Minister of Agriculture in Manitoba, who had just moved to the Touchwood Hills. The Quill Plains had been softened up by the wet season and travel over them was very difficult. Mr. Davis wrote:

> At one place in the middle of the plain we got stuck. We tried to pull the wagon out but failed. The oxen got mired and we unhitched and unloaded the wagon. We had to take the wagon to pieces. We took the wheels off to get it out of the mud. It took us ten days to get across that plain. It was hard work day and night. Along the trail we occasionally met half-breed freighters going down for freight. They were Hudson Bay people.

After crossing the plain they met a freighter named Matheson who afterwards served at Onion Lake as an Anglican missionary. Mr. Davis mentions meeting Mr. Weldon at the old telegraph station at Humboldt, which he says was about five miles west of the present town of Humboldt. Just beyond Humboldt a few miles they passed The Hill of the Cross (Mount Carmel). At that time he says there was a twelve-foot birch cross planted on its summit in memory of a half-breed girl who committed suicide there rather than return to the Red River

Settlement and marry a man she detested. Davis says the girl's name—Miss McKay—was carved on the cross. At Batoche they saw the man after whom the place was named and stated that he had a big store piled up with stuff for trade with the Indians. Davis also states that the trader's real name was Letandre, and that the name Batoche was bestowed upon him by the Indians. The ferry at that time was run by Alex Fisher, a little dark man who afterwards became Lieutenant Governor in Riel's brief regime. They still had to track the barge upstream some distance before attempting to cross the river as they had no ferry cable as yet. From Batoche they took the branch trail leading to Prince Albert and arrived there early in November, having spent about two months on the way.

In June, 1881, Mr. Davis started freighting on his own account with a string of nine carts and oxen. He wrote:

> I used to cart the stuff from Fort Ellice that summer. I walked every step of the way both ways. I drove all nine carts myself, as I was alone. I hitched and unhitched four or five times a day. The harness was a shaganappi harness made out of rawhide. They were made out of oxhide soaked in water and cut in strips. The lead ox was a better judge of a soft place than I was. He was a white ox and his name was Wabascow, which means "white" in Indian. I had him leading with all the rest tied behind, the whole nine on a string. When he came to a soft place he would stop and look up and down and turn up the coulee or down, as the case might be, according to his judgment. He would go very slow crossing a soft place so as not to mire those behind him. His intelligence was really remarkable. He knew his business.

Mr. Davis continued to freight goods from Fort Ellice to Prince Albert in the summer of 1882. The distance was probably about 300 miles by the winding trail and the freighting fee charged was about five cents per pound. At that time coal oil brought five dollars a gallon in Prince Albert, salt twenty-five cents a pound, and needles five cents apiece. The last trip each season—he made three round trips in 1882—was made in cold weather so he had to contend with snow and ice and endure many a cold camp. In addition he had to shoe his oxen, on one trip, to enable them to travel over the hard, frozen ground. However, the enterprise seems to have been remunerative. By 1882 he says that there were mail stations every forty miles along the trail where the mail carriers changed horses.

With the advance of the railway and regular shipping facilities, it became possible to shorten the distance over which goods had to be freighted by cart or wagon to Prince Albert. From 1883 to 1885, Mr. Davis freighted supplies in from South Qu'Appelle instead of Fort Ellice.

STAGE COACHES ON THE CARLTON TRAIL

The following is an account taken from *Saskatchewan and Its People* by John Hawkes (10). It was written by Mr. A. C. Paterson of South Qu'Appelle:

In the fall of 1882 the C.P.R. laid the track through to Regina, and the villages of Indian Head and Qu'Appelle were each nearly the same distance from Fort Qu'Appelle and the Prince Albert trail, so naturally a strong rivalry took place for the base of supplies for the north country. Qu'Appelle had the advantage of a somewhat better road and a few miles nearer and it became the distributing point for the North. Early in '83 a mail contract was awarded to Jim McLean, better known as Flatboat McLean, who shortly afterward transferred the contract to Leeson and Scott, and they kept the line in operation until the Regina and Long Lake and also the Calgary and Edmonton Railways were built.

This stage line was splendidly managed. All along the trail from Qu'Appelle to Prince Albert and in fact to Edmonton, at intervals of forty miles, road houses were erected with a man in charge during the winter months, where not only the stage drivers and their passengers but other travellers who were journeying the long, long, trail, found comfortable lodgings for the night at a reasonable cost. In addition to the mail sacks carried, a considerable amount of express was also handled. A four horse team was always used and frequently two of these teams went out and horses were always changed at the forty-mile stations. The wagons used were

122

especially built, with comfortable seats for passengers and with space for mail and express. This line, together with all the freight for the northern points passing through, made Qu'Appelle one of the busiest points on the railway.

The men who drove on this stage line were expert horsemen and sturdy, resourceful fellows, and many a blizzard they had to fight their way through. Of these, I just recall Jack Art, Ab. Craig and Gordon McIver.

This stage line was well patronized, as Prince Albert even in those days was the centre of an old settlement, and quite a village, besides being headquarters for a large detachment of North West Mounted Police.

MOUNTED POLICE ON THE CARLTON TRAIL

Starting in 1874, and continuing down through the years, the North West Mounted Police made extensive use of the prairie trails until these were superseded by the straight graded roads and highways of the present day. Their first acquaintance with the Carlton Trail was made in the summer of 1874 (44). One detachment of Mounted Police, under Inspector Jarvis, branched off from the remainder of the force at Roche Percée, on August the first, and journeyed to Edmonton via Fort Ellice and Fort Carlton. They reached their destination, after a trying trip, on October the twenty-seventh. On numerous occasions after this, lone riders or groups of these men followed portions of the Old Trail, winter and summer, for many years (Fig. 30).

When Inspector Jarvis and his detachment arrived at Fort Ellice on August the twelfth he proceeded to overhaul his entire equipment and transport. A portion of his force left him to start building winter quarters near Fort Pelly for Commissioner French and certain other detachments of the Mounted Police. As many of his horses and cattle were in very poor condition, some of these were left behind. On August the eighteenth the main body started out for Edmonton on the Carlton Trail. His force now consisted of twenty-three Mounted Police, thirteen

FIG. 31—*This photograph illustrates the uniforms and equipment of the N.C.O.'s of the Mounted Police in the early years of the force.*

half-breeds, thirty horses, and about one hundred cattle. Their supplies were carried in fifty-three carts and twelve wagons. The Qu'Appelle River was crossed the first day. The next day they camped at "The Spring" and prairie chickens figured prominently on their bill of fare. August twenty-first they crossed the Little Cut Arm Creek at a point thirty-one miles from Fort Ellice, so it can be seen that they were not making very fast progress. However, the evening menu was good—hot bread, butter, prairie chicken, veal, bacon, snipe, wild pigeons and tea!

At times it was difficult to find sufficient wood and water for their camps, and a certain amount of time was lost hunting for stray horses or cattle. A day's journey varied from four to twenty-two miles, depending upon the weather and the state of the trail. On August the twenty-eighth they passed the Rev. George McDougall and the Rev. James Nisbet with their wives and a few others traveling to Fort Garry.

On August the thirty-first they camped in the Touchwood Hills and the next day a cold rain fell on them. Wood was collected for crossing the Quill Plains. On the morning of September the second, there was ice on the water buckets! This day they traveled twenty miles and had their first view of a strongly saline lake. Also a herd of antelope was seen. At last a slough of fresh water was reached and camp was made. The evening meal was featured by a plentiful supply of wild ducks. By September the fifth they left the Quill Plains behind. Shortly after this they passed many brigades of hunters, freighters and traders from whom they purchased some pemmican.

On the evening of September the seventh they reached Gabriel's Crossing. The following day they made use of a ferry to take their supplies across the river but they made their cattle swim across it. Fort Carlton was not reached until after dark on September the eleventh, as they were delayed by cold rain and the weak condition of their horses and cattle. The Hudson's Bay factor, Lawrence Clark, was most hospitable. Welcome shelter for the men was found in the fort and the horses were put in its stables. A considerable amount of barley was purchased at this point for the future use of the expedition.

The detachment continued its journey westward on September the twenty-first, but they were greatly harassed by the feeble condition of their livestock, and it was October the twenty-seventh before the leading teams finally reached their winter quarters at Fort Edmonton.

We are indebted to ex-corporal J. C. Donkin (6) for the following glimpses of the progress of a party of twenty "mounties," together with their commanding officer and sergeant, over a portion of the Carlton Trail in December, 1884. The officer and the sergeant were accompanied by their wives. They were being sent north as reinforcements because of the trouble brewing among the Métis and Indians around Batoche. The party set out from Regina, on December the thirteenth, and traveled first to Fort Qu'Appelle where they were detained for several days. Then they proceeded up the Touchwood Trail until they joined the Carlton Trail in the Touchwood Hills, and from this point followed the latter trail to Fort Carlton. They arrived at this post in an exhausted and frost-bitten condition Friday, December the twenty-seventh, after having endured some of the coldest weather on record on the march. But we will take a few extracts from Mr. Donkin's story to illustrate the conditions under which they traveled and camped:

> The order of our procession was as follows: In front was a transport sleigh and a pair of horses, containing tents, camp stoves, and other equipment as well as our rations. Then came our line of jumpers, each driven by one of us in winter uniform. The officer followed us in a superior sort of jumper, a kind of aristocratic box, with varnished sides and high back, in which he could recline at ease. The canvas-covered sleigh, containing the ladies, drawn by a team, brought up the rear.

Of their overnight stop at the Hudson's Bay post in the Touchwood Hills, he said:

> The officer, sergeant, and ladies billeted themselves in the factor's residence, whence the cheerful blaze of a log fire sent a ruddy glow on the snow outside. The stables were ruinous, great holes gaping through the timber of which they were constructed. Here we made our horses as comfortable as we could in such a breezy home. We were quartered in a dilapidated, ancient "shack," near the stables, on the edge of a darksome wood. It was weary work, carrying our bedding and grub through the snow drifts. We stumbled and plunged and fell again and again. There was a cantonment of redskins and half-breeds in the next-door compartment to us. One tall, blanketed savage came out, and stalked weirdly away, his grey figure appeared ghost-like in the wan glamour of the winter's night. Our temporary resting place was not inviting. There was no glass in the antique window frame. The floor had yielded to decay in places, forming many pitfalls for the unwary. The walls were full of yawning holes, admitting every breath of air. We had a wretched night, in spite of our weariness, but after smoking the consolatory calumet, we all fell into an uneasy slumber. Shortly after midnight a huge black form came bounding through the rug we had fixed over the window, landing on the recumbent form of the gentleman from Middlesex, who wildly shrieked, "a bear! . . . a bear!" No doubt, he imaged, in this semi-somnolent state, that the whole menagerie

from the surrounding bush had turned out to make a night of it. It was, however, only a train dog of the Huskie breed, in the service of the fort, who was attracted by the gleam of our pine logs. He made himself at home, after the storm of abuse had passed over.

He continued the tale of hardship:

Sunday, December 21st, was the coldest day on record in the Northwest. The thermometer, on the Saskatchewan, registered minus 62° Fahrenheit; or **ninety-four degrees of frost!** As we passed the lonely hut, in which resided the telegraph operator, the mercury was frozen at minus 45° in the sun. The atmosphere was clear and bright, but cutting as the keenest steel. We kept up our circulation as well as we could, by running alongside the sleighs; this was no easy task in deep snow, with our weight of furs and underclothing. We passed a weasenfaced old Indian, seated in state in his jumper with a great rabbit-skin robe around him; his squaw trudged alongside, and kept hammering the cayuse. We drove by the door of the Indian Agent's house, round which were a collection of painted squaws and braves in all the finery of many-coloured blankets. Here our sleighs were piled with a supply of wood, for right before us, stretching from the foot of the hills, lay the grey expanse of the great Salt Plains.

Reaching the stage-coach station at Hoodoo, north of Humboldt, two days later, they found the house so bare and filthy that the officers and ladies slept in a tent and the men occupied the shack. The trek across the Salt Plains had been a real ordeal and the men bore plentiful marks of their experience. This was Christmas Eve and he wrote:

We slept upon the floor as well as we were able. A disreputable crowd we looked on the following morning! Our fur coats were ornamented with hay seeds and straws. Our chins, noses and cheeks were raw with frostbites, and smeared with vaseline. One man was dyed purple; another blue, and a third was brown. A beard of a fortnight's growth did not add to the many fascinations of our appearance. The ladies entered the hovel to wish us all a very Merry Christmas; and we seemed to afford considerable merriment to them. We all blushed like a lot of idiotic schoolboys; and such was our plight on Christmas Day.

127

The next night they slept in Philippe Garnot's hostelry at Batoche after dining on steak and rice pudding. Besides the hotel there was, at that time, a Catholic church, a post office, a blacksmith's shop and a few residences including that of Batoche, which had many windows and was painted a pale green. Also, according to Donkin, Gabriel Dumont had a saloon at Batoche, a small low-roofed log building plastered with mud. In it French billiards was played, nauseous hop-beer was imbibed and much violent sedition was talked by the Métis who frequented the place. Many other settlers had homes strung along the river above and below the village.

Finally the troop reached Fort Carlton (Fig. 31) and received a rousing welcome there. Most of them stayed to reinforce the garrison of police at Carlton, but Donkin went on to Prince Albert, where he remained all through the rebellion, helping to protect the settlers at that point. Before proceeding with his account of his return journey to Regina the following August we will mention several incidents that occurred along the Carlton Trail during the rebellion of 1885.

THE MOUNTED POLICE "GIVE THE MÉTIS THE SLIP"

After receiving an urgent call for further reinforcements from Superintendent Crozier of Carlton, Commissioner Irvine set out from Regina on March the eighteenth with ninety men and the necessary horses and sleighs to convey them (44). They passed through Fort Qu'Appelle on the nineteenth, crossed the Quill Plains on the twenty-second, and camped that night at a stage-coach station six miles north of the telegraph station at Humboldt. On March the twenty-third they reached a station called Hoodoo, and found that it had been sacked by the Métis. However, they camped there for the night. Having heard that the Métis were prepared to stop them at Batoche, Irvine led his men another six or seven miles along the trail and then made a detour to the northeast and north which took them around the western border of the Birch Hills and across the South Saskatchewan River at Agnew's Ferry and then on to Prince Albert, where they were received with great rejoicing by the settlers and police stationed at that isolated colony. Thus they completed a journey of about 300 miles in sub-zero weather in seven days.

FIG. 32—*Fort Carlton as it was in 1872.*

THE BATTLE OF DUCK LAKE

As fate would have it, Superintendent Crozier and his force of about one hundred men were drawn into a fight with a larger force of Métis on March the twenty-sixth, just a matter of hours before Commissioner Irvine arrived at Carlton with another force of about equal strength (44). Crozier had sent out a party of seventeen men with sleighs to bring in some supplies that Hillyard Mitchell had left in the trading store at Duck Lake. Gabriel Dumont met them with a larger body of men at his command and turned them back. After consultation with his officers and those of the Prince Albert volunteers, Crozier started out with a force of fifty-three Mounted Police and forty volunteers and a small field gun. They traveled in sleighs and, as the snow was still deep, it was very difficult to maneuver his force except on the packed trail.

About two miles west of the Duck Lake store on the Carlton Trail they were confronted by the Métis. The enemy attempted to envelope Crozier's force while an Indian engaged Crozier and his interpreter in a fake parley. Firing broke out almost immediately and after half an hour's severe fighting the Mounted Police and volunteers retired with a loss of twelve killed or mortally wounded men and eleven less seriously injured. Some of the dead and the field gun were abandoned on the site of the battle.

Half an hour after the return of Crozier's force, Irvine and his men arrived at Carlton. Since it was considered more important to protect the settlers at Prince Albert than to hold Fort Carlton, the combined force made good their retreat to Prince Albert on the following day. In the excitement of leaving, a fire was started accidentally and much of the post was burned.

THE TRAIL BECOMES A MILITARY HIGHWAY

In April, 1885, a portion of the Old Trail was utilized by most of the troops of General Middleton in their march to attack the Métis at Batoche. These troops came from Winnipeg and Eastern Canada to South Qu'Appelle by train, and from that point, followed the Touchwood Trail via Fort Qu'Appelle to the place in the hills where it joined the Carlton Trail. From Humboldt they went west on the Battleford Trail along the telegraph line to Clark's Crossing. To this point the Midland Battalion came down the South Saskatchewan River from Saskatchewan Landing on the steamer *Northcote*. Part of the battalion was assigned to guard the stores at Clark's Crossing while

Fig. 33—*The site of Fort Carlton as it appeared in November, 1954. In the foreground weeds around several of the old cellars are visible. In the background at right a remnant of the Carlton Trail may be seen climbing from the benchland to the plateau above.*

the remainder pushed on and joined Middleton's forces at Fish Creek.

The following account is taken from a booklet entitled *The Riel Rebellion 1885,* published by the Witness Printing House of Montreal (1):

The first advance was made on April 9th by a detachment of the 90th (Winnipeg) and thirty scouts under Captain French. They reached Touchwood on April 10th, by which date the whole division, composed of the remainder of the 90th (Winnipeg), the first half of C Company, the Winnipeg Field Battery and A Battery (Quebec), brigaded under Colonel Montizambert, the 10th Grenadiers (Toronto), and Boulton's Mounted Scouts, under Colonel Grasseit, were on the way between Qu'Appelle and Touchwood. Four hundred horse teams transported the baggage and supplies of the forces. From Touchwood to Humboldt, a station where a large quantity of Government stores lay, which it was feared might be seized by the enemy, the distance was 78 miles, the weather was bad and salt bogs had to be passed, but it was done in four days. Though only 63 miles from Batoche, the rebels had not disturbed the Humboldt settlement. There the trail forks; one path continuing almost due north to Batoche, the other leading west along the telegraph route to Clark's Crossing on the South Saskatchewan River. The trail to Clark's Crossing was followed, and the advance force camped for the night 25 miles west of Humboldt at Vermilion Lake [Muskiki Lake]. Fire signals blazed on the hills to the north and the west, showing that the troops had reached the enemy's country, their presence was known and their movements watched. At Clark's Crossing there were a couple of ferry scows, and as it was but forty-five miles from Batoche it was believed the rebels would seize it, destroy the scows, and attempt to prevent the troops from crossing. Next morning, with the intention of anticipating them, a dash over the thirty-eight miles was made in eight hours by French's Scouts, C Company and a few men of A Battery, and Clark's Crossing was safe. Though the men had marched the whole distance in eleven days — had travelled, wet or dry, twelve hours, averaging twenty-one miles a day — they were impatient to push on to Batoche.

However, the troops had to put up with considerable delay before Batoche was reached and captured. First they had to wait until the remaining units arrived from Qu'Appelle. They started northeast along the river on April the twenty-third and the next day fought the engagement at Fish Creek. Following this fight there was another long delay to await the coming of the steamer *Northcote* with reinforcements and supplies from Saskatchewan Landing near Swift Current. Finally on May the seventh they resumed their march and after several days of fighting defeated the Métis defenders and captured Louis Riel, their political leader. However, their doughty military leader, Gabriel Dumont, who formerly operated the ferry at Gabriel's Crossing, escaped to Montana. Rifle pits were strategically placed on either side of the Carlton Trail where it came into Batoche from the east. Apparently the Métis had expected the troops to attack from that quarter and had prepared a warm reception for them. During the battle the steamer, *Northcote,* ran down the river past the village with some troops on board. Besides peppering the boat with rifle fire from the high wooded banks, the Métis lowered the steel ferry cable and tore off part of the boat's superstructure and nearly stopped her completely, but she pulled free and passed on down the river to safety. The village of Batoche was somewhat battered during the battle, and sixty years later bullet marks could still be seen on the tower of the church there. As for Fort Carlton, it never rose from its ashes, and it ceased to be a stopping place on the way to Edmonton (Fig. 32).

CORPORAL DONKIN RETURNS TO REGINA

The following autumn, Corporal Donkin returned to Regina in company with the same Mounted Police officer and his wife with whom he had traveled north the previous winter. They traveled by wagon, following the trail through the wooded sand hills to St. Laurent and along the river to Batoche. The autumn air was very pleasant and redolent with the smoke of bush and prairie fires. As they traveled they shot enough prairie chickens and wild ducks to keep themselves supplied with fresh meat. Donkin states that the ferry cable at Batoche had been removed but a ferry was in operation propelled in the ancient manner with oars. The village of Batoche looked woe-begone and deserted. Its houses still showed the marks of war. The remains of Middleton's zareba and the rifle pits of the Métis were still fresh when Donkin passed them that pleasant autumn day, but all was calm and peaceful around the place.

They turned south at Batoche and followed the river to Gabriel's Crossing and took the newer branch of the Carlton Trail to Humboldt. On the way they made camp for the night in a delightful spot by a pretty little lake with bluffs of poplar and birch to shelter them from the wind. During the night

Donkin was suddenly roused from his slumber by the wild yapping of a pack of coyotes close to their camp. His description of the serenade is worth repeating:

It must have been, I imagine, by the moon's position, about one o'clock in the morning, when I was suddenly awakened by the most unearthly row I ever heard. Evidently a Home Rule party of coyotes were holding an indignation meeting somewhere. First there was a peal of demon laughter, followed by a wild, despairing shriek, mingled with a howl from another portion of the orchestra. A series of sharp yelps — probably taking the place of our Hear! hear! — were now introduced, which were succeeded by another tumultuous burst of laughing. A grand finale of yells, shrieks, howls, barks, and screams of hilarity wound up the entertainment: it was evidently a great success. The cry of the coyote, breaking in upon the startled ear of night, as it invariably does, is about the most hideous I ever listened to.

FIG. 34—*A small slough in the Touchwood Hills. Seen in early spring when the poplar buds were bursting.*

Of their camp in the Touchwood Hills he wrote:

We camped in a lovely spot — a gem of woodland beauty, in the
rich setting of the fall. Groves of magnificent timber climbed the
slopes, while a fairy lake peeped through the tangled screen
[Fig. 33]. We lay awake for some time under the starlight, smoking
and spinning yarns of bygone times.

What a strong contrast to their winter camps in which all were
cold and miserable! But cold or warm, wet or dry, the mounties
(Fig. 34) continued to follow their paths of duty for many long
years over the winding trails of the Canadian Northwest.

HIGHWAY ROBBERY ON THE TRAIL

The Carlton Trail has only one tale of highway robbery
connected with it (10). This incident occurred on July 18, 1886.
At a point between the Salt Plains and Humboldt the stage,
carrying the mail and also carrying J. F. Betts and a farmer
named Fiddler from Prince Albert, was held up by an armed
robber. The following is an account of the affair given by the
stage driver, John Art, at the trial of the hold-up man:

About twenty-five miles south of Humboldt, and in a bluffy country,
a voice out of the bluff shouted "stop!" I looked and saw a man
on the edge of the bluff pointing a double-barrelled gun. The man
next said "Hands up!" I threw my hands up. He said "Jump off
your wagon!" The two passengers jumped off but I did not. He
then said "Jump or I'll shoot!" I jumped. He then ordered us
away from the wagon and told us to get down on our knees,
I got down, and he tied my hands with a bed cord. I saw him have
a revolver in his hand. He tied Mr. Betts and made Fiddler drive
the wagon. He got up on the wagon and said "Now driver, you
will save yourself some time by telling me where the box with
the lock on it is." I told him I did not know of any box. When
he could not find the box, he cut open the mail bags, and put
some of the letters in his shirt. He then said, "I am done with you
fellow." I said I felt a bit cheap to have one man hold up three.
He said, "You needn't feel cheap, for I and my partner held up
a bigger crowd than you this morning." The robber used Mr.
Bett's knife to cut open the mail bags and took his roll of money

135

at first but later gave it back saying that he didn't want his
private money. When he was through the robber backed away
and disappeared behind the bluff.

It turned out that he had robbed a party of four campers
the previous morning.

Subsequently a man named Garnet, who ran a ferry at St.
Louis on the South Saskatchewan River, was convicted of the
robbery and sentenced to fourteen years in the Stony Mountain
Penitentiary.

FIG. 35—*Mounties and helpers at one of their outposts.*

PRAIRIE FIRES ALONG THE CARLTON TRAIL

A number of travelers who made use of the Carlton Trail
have mentioned briefly the prairie fires and their destructive
influence on tree growth. Mr. McKenzie, who was in charge of
the last Hudson's Bay Company post in the Touchwood Hills,

has left a vivid account (30a) of an extensive fire that swept through the Touchwood Hills while he was in charge of the trading post there.

Mr. McKenzie had been on an inspection trip to the Nut Lake post with his superior, Mr. Archibald McDonald, and the two had separated near Fishing Lake. Mr. McDonald was going on to Fort Pelly and Mr. McKenzie was returning home with a team and buggy. It was in the autumn and the weather had been very dry. Most of the sloughs were dried up and the vegetation in the meadows, marshes, and woods was thoroughly desiccated. This is his story:

I had not driven many miles when all about me ashes began to fall in flakes like a snow shower. The wind was blowing hard, an undoubted sign that a big prairie fire was in action. Coming on to a ridge I could see smoke in the distance, in the direction of Touchwood. Prairie fires were quite common in the fall, and as a rule we did not give them any particular attention, but this fall everything was dried up and the grass was unusually long everywhere on account of the heavy rains in the early part of the season. As I drove towards it I could see that the fire was extensive, the whole country seemed to be in flames, and the fire was travelling with great rapidity with an increasing gale blowing. The heat was getting intense. The whole atmosphere seemed to be on fire. Smoke had gotten so dense that the sun was completely obscured. Bundles of grass all aflame carried by the fierce wind were falling all around me, and the wind was nearly as hot as a furnace blast. I came on to another small ridge, driving as fast as the horses could go, the poor beasts were now in a lather of foam and sweat. I could see the flames and hear their roar. I was entirely surrounded by fire, and at very close quarters from this particular one, right in front of me. The horses were frightened and so was I, but there was no time to lose if I was to save them and myself. The fire was travelling at the rate of fifteen to twenty-five miles an hour and where the grass was very long in dry sloughs it was making much faster time. I jumped out and set fire to the grass in my immediate vicinity and got the team and myself on the burnt ground. By this time the smoke was nearly suffocating us. I got in front of my team, put my blanket over their heads, and

137

got my own head in with theirs and kept most of the smoke out of our lungs, otherwise we should have perished. It was one of the worst prairie fires, and the closest call I had ever experienced. That arm of the fire passed us with a roar, licking up everything in its path. There was no more danger of being burned to death but the intense heat still in the air was hard to endure, and the team was very restless when I took the blanket off our heads. The smoke had partially gone to leeward, and here the team and I stood alone on a ridge in the midst of a black, burned wilderness, that had been so beautiful a few hours before, with the grasses and flowers waving and rejoicing in their most beautiful autumn tints.

Water was what myself and the horses wanted now, but I knew there was none within three or four miles of us, and then it was only a small spring, which I might not be able to find, as it was some distance off the trail, and the fire had altered the appearance of the whole face of the country.

The fire that I had just come through had started in the great salt plain, between the big Touchwood and Humboldt, sweeping right through the Quill plain over which I was then travelling. There were numerous other fires to the east and south of me as I could see by the smoke, and this section I had still to pass through. I was also very anxious about my family at the Post as I could see heavy smoke in that direction and I was still about twenty-five miles from home.

All this had taken place in a much less time than it has taken me to write it down, although it appeared hours to me at the time. Water was what we now wanted, and we wanted it badly. The horses were quite badly singed about the head and breasts, and I had parted with my own eyebrows and eyelashes, and was blistered a little on the face and hands.

I pulled on to the trail again, the horses were not feeling very gay so I let them walk along slowly for a mile or so, and then started them on a slow trot, but gave them their heads, did not tighten the reins at all, as I was in hopes they would fork off, when we came near where the spring should be, as I was sure it was still ahead of us. All land marks had been obliterated by the fire.

We had gone quite a distance, but not nearly as far as I had thought, and I was beginning to despair, when all at once the team left the trail. I said nothing to them, but let them go their own way. I knew there was a little clump of bushes where the spring was, but I could see nothing as far as I could look ahead but burnt prairie. However, I let them go, as they seemed willing and were increasing their pace in a straight bee line for some place. I looked back and could see the buggy track as straight as a line behind us. In a few minutes I saw a few red foxes ahead of us, and some badgers and skunks, that had come through the fire; some of them were pretty well scorched, in fact their pelts would be useless for that season, and many of them would not live through the winter. Foxes that were burned like these were what we called "Samsons," and were useless.

All this passed through my mind in an instant, when a couple of black tail deer bounced past within twenty yards of us. They had also been through the fire, and were badly singed. They disappeared over a ridge a short distance ahead. I was so thirsty by this time that I could only speak to my team with difficulty. The team started to trot as the deer passed us and just over the ridge lay the spring with a lot of these crippled and burned wild

FIG. 36—*Eskdale School and pupils as seen in 1910. The logs for this building were hauled over the Touchwood Trail from the Touch-wood Hills. The school was situated nine miles south of Leross, Sask.*

139

animals standing and lying near it. The poor things did not seem at all frightened at our arrival and just watched us from a short distance. We were all pilgrims in distress. I unhitched the team but allowed them only a few mouthfuls of water and took very little myself. After a little while I gave the horses all they would drink and also drank as much as I wanted myself.

I hitched up again and started in a diagonal course until I struck the trail. I saw several foxes and prairie wolves heading for the spring. It seemed to be the only water in that part of the country at that time, and was surely a blessing to the wild animals in that vicinity. It was certainly the most precious sight that I had seen in years. I took my tea kettle full of it in the rig with me, and took a sip of it now and again.

The wind had changed and the fires were now travelling in all directions, but towards evening it was not blowing so hard, though still very hot. The fire had crossed that trail in many places, and I had to drive through it, both the horses and myself being pretty well scorched several times. Towards sundown my team got competely played out. They could not even go at a slow walk. I unhitched them, took their harness off and rubbed them all over. There was nothing for them to eat, so we had to try it again after half an hour's rest. I saw that the fire was in round the Post but it was not the same fire that I had been in all day, it had come upon them from the east. The fires all around looked much worse as it began to get dark. I was about three miles from the Post and had now to go through fire all the way. I was sure from the look of things that the Post and everything else was burned, as I could see nothing but fire in all the bluffs around where the Post was. I don't know how the horses or myself made the last mile and a half, but when I got there the Post was still standing, although everything was burned right up to the buildings.

My family were all safe and so was Jamie Slater. The fire had jumped the fire guards round the Post many times, but they had been able to combat it from the buildings and stables. They had been fighting it from about noon. Mrs. McKenzie had gathered all the Indians from the reserve who could come to help, and they had certainly all worked like niggers. The fire was still being watched but all the burning was going on outside the plowed fireguards now. They had taken a lot of furniture out of the house, and piled it up in the garden, the youngest baby in the cradle among

140

the pile. Mrs. McKenzie was a sight to behold. She had been out all day directing the Indians first at one point and then at another whenever the fire would jump the guards. She was certainly a tired woman, but had saved the Fort and her children with the aid of Slater and the Indians.

The fire in the bluffs burned for several days, and in many of the sloughs the earth was on fire and burned all winter. Several people lost their lives in some parts. Cattle and horses died from burns; many hay stacks were destroyed. Rabbits, prairie chicken and many of the smaller fur bearing animals were burned. It was the most disastrous all over prairie fire that had been in the country during my time.

FIG. 37—*Municipal road through rolling park country between Dysart and Lestock, Sask.*

THE TRAIL BECOMES DESERTED

With the completion of the branch railway line from Regina to Prince Albert in 1890, freighting over the old Trail from South Qu'Appelle to Prince Albert ceased, and traffic over the Carlton Trail degenerated into short-distance hauling where the trail happened to lead from new towns to the homes of ranchers and farmers. For instance, many of the German-American immigrants, who in 1903 established St. Peter's Colony, stretching from Bruno to Engelfeld, came by train to Rosthern and made use of the Carlton Trail to get from Gabriel's Crossing to their homesteads. Heavy wagons, demo-crats, and buggies replaced the carts and buckboards of earlier times on the Trail in summer. In winter, when snow covered the ground, sleighs and jumpers came into general use. These new vehicles brought in the settters' effects from the nearest town after they had arrived by boxcar from far-off homes in Eastern Canada, Europe, or the United States. Then the neces-sary lumber and other building materials were hauled to the homesteads to erect houses and stables, unless the newcomer constructed his first farm buildings of logs or sod. Later the trails were utilized to take out the first trickle of grain as the new fields began to produce, and the giant sentinels of the new villages, the grain elevators, appeared in increasing numbers. At this stage in the development of new communities, building materials were hauled in for the first schools (Fig. 36) and churches, although in many cases church services were held in school houses until the homesteaders were more permanently established. At times, for a short period, supplies were freighted from established railway lines to construction gangs working on newer lines. An example of this was seen by the writer in 1908 when the Grand Trunk Pacific Railway was being built through the Touchwood Hills.

Gradually municipal roads (Fig. 37) became established on the allowances intended for the purpose, fences were erected and the traffic was diverted from the old trails to these new-fangled roads. Traffic no longer wound in leisurely curves around bluff and slough, but plunged doggedly ahead in a

142

FIG. 38—*Fort Ellice in its later years. Note the Red River cart near the building on the left.*

straight line even though in some of the rougher districts "heaven and earth" had to be moved to make this possible.

The old Trail with its accompanying telegraph line enjoyed special immunity for many years in certain parts. The writer followed it from Fort Qu'Appelle to a point fifteen miles north of Lipton in 1906, and as late as 1925 he traveled over one branch of it from Bruno to Gabriel's Crossing. Even now it is followed for part of the way from Duck Lake to the Carlton Ferry, and it can be traced across the Poor Man Indian reserve north of Punnichy. However, for the most part it has been blocked by fences and fields, and has largely disappeared from the sight and memory of men. Only the faces of real oldtimers light up with an expression of understanding and affection when its name is mentioned nowadays.

BIBLIOGRAPHY

1. ANONYMOUS — *The Riel Rebellion 1885*. Witness Printing House. Montreal, 1885.

2. BUTLER, CAPT. W. F. — *The Great Lone Land*. S. Low, Marston, Low and Searle. London, 1872.

3. CHEADLE, DR. W. B. — *Journal of a Trip Across Canada 1862-63*. Graphic Publishers Ltd. Ottawa, 1931.

4. COWIE, ISAAC — *The Company of Adventurers*. William Briggs. Toronto, 1913.

5. DALY, T. MAYNE — *Description of the Province of Manitoba*. Printed by the Queen's Printer, Ottawa. 1893.

6. DONKIN, JOHN G. — *Trooper and Redskin*. S. Low, Marston, Searle and Rivington. London, 1889.

7. FEATHERSTONHAUGH, R. C. — *Royal Canadian Mounted Police*. Carrick and Evans Inc., New York, 1938.

8. GORDON, REV. D. M. — *Mountain and Prairie*. S Low, Marston, Searle and Rivington., London, 1880.

9. GRANT, REV. GEORGE M. — *Ocean to Ocean, Sandford Fleming's Expedition Through Canada in 1872*. S. Low, Marston, Low and Searle, London, 1873.

10. HAWKES, JOHN — *Saskatchewan and Its People, Vols. I and II*. S. J. Clarke Publishing Co., Chicago-Regina, 1924.

11. HAWORTH, P. L. — *Trail Makers of the North-West*. Harcourt, New York, 1921.

12. HIND, HENRY YOULE — *Narrative of the Canadian Red River Exploring Expedition of 1857 and of the Assiniboine and Saskatchewan Exporing Expedition of 1858, Vol. I.* — Longman, Green, Longman and Roberts, London, 1860.

13. HUGHES, KATHERINE — *Father Lacombe*. Wm. Briggs, Toronto, 1911.

14. JARVIS, E. W. — *Report of Canadian Pacific Railway up to 1877, by Sandford Fleming, Engineer-in-Chief. Appendix H, pp. 145-161, 1874-5*. MacLean, Roger and Co., Ottawa, 1877.

15. KANE, PAUL — *The Wanderings of an Artist Among the Indians of North America*. The Radisson Society of Canada, Toronto, 1925.

16. LOVERIDGE, A. J. — *The Story of My Life*. Unpublished manuscript, Grenfell, Sask., 1950.

17. MACBETH, R. G. — *Policing the Plains*. Hodder and Stoughton Ltd., London and New York, 1921.

18. MACOUN, JOHN — *Report of the Canadian Pacific Railway up to 1874 by Sandford Fleming, Engineer-in-Charge*. MacLean, Roger & Co., Ottawa, 1874.

19. MACOUN, JOHN — *Report of the Canadian Pacific Railway up to 1877, by Sandford Fleming, Engineer-in-Charge. Appendix X. Description of Canada Between Lake Superior and Rocky Mountains*. MacLean, Roger & Co., Ottawa, 1877.

20. MACOUN, JOHN — *Report of the Canadian Pacific Railway, 1880, by Sandford Fleming, Engineer-in-Charge. Appendix No. 14, pp. 235-245*. MacLean, Roger & Co., Ottawa, 1880.

21. MACOUN, JOHN — *Manitoba and the Great North-west*. The World Publishing Co., Guelph, Ontario, 1882.

22. MACDONALD, J. S. — *The Dominion Telegraph*. Canadian Northwest Historical Society. Vol. I, No. VI. Battleford, Sask., 1930.

23. MACDONELL, REV. W. A. — *The Life - Story of the Rev. James Nisbet, Pioneer Presbyterian Missionary to the Indians of the Saskatchewan*. Unpublished manuscript, Archives of St. Andrew's College, United Church of Canada, University of Saskatchewan, Saskatoon, Sask.

24. McDOUGALL, JOHN — *Forest, Lake and Prairie — Twenty Years of Frontier Life in Western Canada, 1842-62*. William Briggs, Toronto, 1895.

25. McDOUGALL, JOHN — *Saddle, Sled and Snowshoe — Pioneering on the Saskachewan in the Sixties*. William Briggs, Toronto, 1896.

26. McDOUGALL JOHN — *Pathfinding on Plain and Prairie*. William Briggs, Toronto, 1898.

27. McDOUGALL, JOHN — *In the Days of the Red River Rebellion*. William Briggs, Toronto, 1903.

28. McDOUGALL, JOHN — *On Western Trails in the Early Seventies*. William Briggs, Toronto, 1911.

29. McDOUGALL, JOHN — *George Millward McDougall, the Pioneer, Patriot and Missionary*. William Briggs, Toronto, 1888.

30. McKELLAR, REV. HUGH — *Presbyterian Pioneer Ministers*. Murray Printing Co. Ltd., Toronto, 1924.

30a McKenzie, N. M. W. J. — *The Men of the Hudson's Bay Company*. Times-Journal Presses, Fort William, Ontario, 1921.

31. Merk, Frederick — *Fur Trade and Empire, George Simpson's Diary 1824-1825*. Harvard University Press, Cambridge, 1931.

32. Moore, Rev. Wm. — *Report on the Condition and Working of the Prince Albert Presbyterian Mission to the Indians on the Saskatchewan*. A. S. Woodburn, Ottawa, 1873.

33. Morton, Arthur S. — *A History of the Canadian West to 1870-1871*. Thomas Nelson & Sons, Ltd., Toronto, 1939.

34. Mulvaney, C. P. — *The History of the North-west Rebellion of 1885*. A. H. Hovey & Co., Toronto, 1886.

35. Nelson, H. S. — *Four Months Under Arms*. Nelson Daily News Printing Department, Nelson, B.C. (194-).

36. Oliver, Edmund H. — *The Presbyterian Church in Saskatchewan 1866-1881*. Trans. Royal Soc. Canada, 3rd Series, Sec. II, Vol. XXVIII, 1934.

37. Palliser, Capt. John — *Exploration in British North America, 1857-1860*. H. M. Stationery Office, London, 1863.

38. Sandercock, W. Clark — *Where History Was Made*. Canadian Geographical Journal, Vol. VII, No. 4, 153-162, October, 1933.

39. Simpson, Sir George — *Narrative of a Journey Round the World*. *Vol. I*. Henry Colburn Publishers, London, 1847.

40. Sissons, C. K. — *John Kerr*. Oxford University Press, Toronto, 1946.

41. Southesk, James Carnegie, Earl of — *Saskatchewan and the Rocky Mountains*. Jas. Campbell & Son, Toronto, 1875.

42. Sutherland, Rev. A. — *A Summer in Prairie Land*. Methodist Book and Publishing House, Toronto, 1881.

43. Trow, Jas. — *Manitoba and North-west Territories*. Dept Agric., Ottawa, 1878.

44. Turner, John Peter — *The North-west Mounted Police 1873-1893*. *Vols. I and II*. King's Printer, Ottawa, 1950.

45. Wade, W. M. — *The Overlanders of '62*. Government Printer, Victoria, B.C., 1931.

46. White, Hon. Thomas — *Descriptions of the Townships of the North-west Territories (between 2nd and 3rd mer.)*. MacLean, Roger & Co., Ottawa, 1886.

47. WHITE, HON. THOMAS — *Descriptions of the Townships of the North-west Territories (between 3rd and 4th mer.).* MacLean, Roger & Co., Ottawa, 1886.

48. WILLIAMS, W. H. — *Manitoba and the North-west.* Hunter, Rose & Co., Toronto, 1882.

INDEX

Canadian Pacific Railway, 51, 59, 74, 89, 94, 103, 122
Cariboo, 34, 61
Carlton Ferry, 143
Carlton House, 47
Carmel, Sask., 91
Carruthers, Mr., 85
Charing Cross, Ont., xi
Cheadle, Dr. W. B., 36-39
Child's Mountain, 79
Churchill River brigade, 11
Clark, Lawrence, (H.B.Co. factor), 59, 60, 70, 81, 106, 125
Clarke, Rev. T. A., 118
Clark's Crossing, 74, 108, 130, 132
Columbia River valley, 17, 23
Connor, Mr., 43, 44
Cowley, Archdeacon, 78
Craig, Ab., 123
Crowfoot, Blackfoot chief, 108
Crozier, Capt. (N.W.M.P.), 69, 70, 128, 129, 130
Cudworth, 53
Cut Arm Creek, 41, 86
Cypress Hills, 65
Dafoe, 73, 101
Dana, 9
Daniel, John, 116
Davis, Sen. T. O., 120-122
Dawson, Dr. G. M., 88
Day Star, Chief, 88
de Merse, Mons., 22
Derwentwater, 37, 38
Description of the Province of Manitoba, 2
Descriptions of the Townships of the Northwest Territories, 99
DeWinton, Col., 105
Deville, E., 100
Donaldson, S. J., 87
Donkin, J. C., 125, 126, 127, 128, 133-135
Duck Lake, vii, 1, 8, 114, 116, 129, 130, 143
Duck Lake, battle of, 70, 129-130
Dumont, Gabriel, 8, 61, 81, 128, 129, 132
Dunomais, Pierre, 17
Dysart, 62, 141
Eagle Hill Creek, 29, 39, 116
Eagle Hills, 25
Edmonton, *see* Fort Edmonton
Ellisboro, 94
Engelfeld, 142
Eskdale School, 139
Fenwood, 100
Fiddler, Mr., 135
Field, Edward, 102, 103

File Hills, 72
Fish (storekeeper), 111, 112
Fish Creek, Sask., 13, 132
Fisher, Alex, 121
Fishing Lake, 103, 137
Fleming, Sanford, 45, 51-59, 66
Flett, George, 47
Fort à la Corne, 9, 26
Fort Benton, U.S.A., 108
Fort Carlton, 1, 8, 10, 11, 12, 13, 17, 18, 19, 20, 21, 24, 25, 29, 30, 36, 37, 38, 39, 45, 46, 47, 48, 49, 50, 51, 59, 60, 62, 64, 68, 69, 70, 76, 81, 88, 100, 104, 105, 106, 116, 117, 123, 125, 126, 128, 129, 130, 131, 133
Fort Edmonton, 11, 21, 22, 24, 29, 34, 39, 40, 45, 46, 51, 60, 63, 73, 74, 88, 99, 100, 108, 109, 114, 118, 119, 122, 123, 125
Fort Ellice, 4, 12, 13, 18, 23, 24, 25, 27, 29, 35, 37, 39, 41, 42, 49, 54, 61, 62, 65, 71, 76, 77, 78, 85, 88, 93, 94, 99, 100, 101, 102, 104, 108, 110, 111, 121, 122, 123, 124, 143
Fort Garry, 1, 11, 12, 17, 20, 21, 23, 24, 26, 29, 30, 34, 36, 40, 42, 45, 48, 51, 52 56, 60, 70, 100, 104, 124, *see also,* Winnipeg
Fort Macleod, 108
Fort McLeod, 63
Fort Pelly, 23, 24, 30, 65, 72, 74, 77, 93, 103, 123, 137
Fort Pitt, 17, 22, 24, 29, 30, 46, 51, 60, 81
Fort Qu'Appelle, 25, 45, 76, 79, 94, 99, 104, 111, 112, 113, 122, 125, 128, 130, 143
Fort St. James, 63
Fort Saskatchewan, 118
Fort Walsh, ix, 65
Fourmond, Father, 82, 83
Franklin, Sir John, 23
French, Capt. (N.W.M.P.), 77, 123, 132
Gabriel's Crossing, 8, 61, 76, 81, 88, 101, 105, 125, 132, 133, 142, 143
Ganges River, 17
Garnett, Mr., 136
Garnot, Philippe, (hostelry), 128
George, Rev. and Mrs., 42
Gladstone, Man., 3
Glen, Rowan, ix
Goose Lake, 29
Gordon Indian Reserve, 65, 76, 80, 113
Gordon, Rev. Daniel M., 88, 89
Grandin, Bishop, 46
Grand Trunk Pacific Railway, vii, 4, 75, 142
Grant, Rev. George M., 51, 52, 67
Grassett, Col., 131
Great Salt Plains, 5, 73, 80. 127, 138
Gregg, Man., 3
Grenfell, ix, 93
Griesbach, Inspector, (N.W.M.P.), 65, 79

Gwynne, Mr., 89, 90
Hamilton Colonization Company, 88
Hand Hills, 65
Hardisty, Richard, 119
Harriett, Mr., 22
Hart, Prof. Thomas, 109
Hawkes, John, 122
Heart Hill, 26, 27, 80
Hector, Dr., 13, 24, 78
Herchmer, Col., 104, 105, 118
High Bluff, 85, 110
Hill of the Cross, 83, 90, 91, 120, *also see* Mount Carmel
Hind, Prof. H. Y., 25-28, 50
Holmes, Mr. (land seeker), 113-114
Hoodoo, 102, 127, 128
Hoover, Mr., 26, 28
Horetsky, Mr., 57, 63
Hubbard, 100
Hudson Bay, 9
"Hudson's Bay blankets," 42
Hudson's Bay Company, 8, 9, 10, 12, 17, 20, 21, 28, 36, 77, 91, 106
Hudson's Bay Hill, 94
Humboldt, vii, 5, 8, 43, 59, 65, 74, 75, 76, 87, 88, 101, 102, 110, 114, 120,
     127, 128, 130, 131, 133, 135, 138
Indian Head, 122
Irvine, Commissioner, (N.W.M.P.), 128, 129, 130
Jarvis, E. W., 59-63, 91
Jarvis, Inspector, (N.W.M.P.), 123
Jeannie, Rev. Baird's sister, 114
Ka-Kake, 42
Kane, Paul, 20-23, 29
Katepwa Lake, 41
Kelliher, 100
Kildonan, 46, 47
King, W. F., 111
Kutawa, 75, 100, 102
Lac la Biche, 41
Lacombe, Father, 11, 13, 24, 46, 51
Laird, Lt. Gov., 84, 116, 118
Lake Manitoba, 4, 51, 74, 102, 103
Lake Ste. Ann's, 24
Lake Winnipeg, 12, 21, 23, 40
Lake Winnipegosis, 51
Langham, 74
Lanigan, 5, 12
La Ronde, Mr., 39
Last Mountain, 27, 80
Last Mountain Lake, 27, 28, 65, 72
Laurie, Mr., 118
Leamy, Const., (N.W.M.P.), 105

Melville, 4
Messiter, Mr., 36, 38, 39
Mickle, Mr. (land seeker), 113, 114
Middleton, General, 130, 131, 133
Milton, Lord, 36-39
Minitchinass (Solitary Hill), 50
Minnedosa, 3, 4, 103, 110
Minnedosa River, 3, 68, *see also* Little Saskatchewan River
Minnesota, 11
Minnesota massacre, 107
Missouri Coteau, 13, 29, 49
Missouri River, 2, 13, 21, 54
Mistawasis, chief (Big Child), 106, 107
Mitchell, Hillyard, 129
Montana, 132
Moore, Capt., 82, 87
Moose Jaw, 65
Moose Mountains, 65
Morleyville, 40
Moss, Mr., 76
Motherwell, Ont., 109
Motizambert, Col., 131
Mount Carmel (Round Hill), 57, 90, 91, 120, *see also* Hill of the
    Cross
Mount Rundle, 21
Muskiki Lake (Vermilion Lake), 76, 132
Neepawa, 4
Nisbet, Mrs. James, 47
Nisbet, Rev. James, 26, 46-48, 110, 124
Nolin, Charles, 120
Northcote, steamboat, 107, 130, 132, 133
North Saskatchewan River, 1, 3, 10, 22, 23, 24, 40, 45, 46, 47, 74, 82, 116
North West Company, 10
North West Mounted Police (Mounties), vii, 64, 65, 69, 70, 104, 105,
    112, 123-130
Northwest Territories, 1, 64, 65, 75, 88, 89, 103, 110, 117
Norway House, 21, 40
Nut Lake post, 137
Oak Lake, Man., 94
Oak Point, 67
Oberon, 3
Ocean to Ocean, 67
Ogilvie, Mr., 71
Ogilvie, W., 100
O'Keefe, D. C., 93
Old Wives Lake, 65
Onion Lake, 120
Oregon Trail, 9
Ottawa, 64, 88, 99
Palliser, Capt. John, 13, 23-25